Velma —
A little
Present for your Soul
Nancy Mau
2001

The Beckoning Song
of
Your Soul

A Guidebook for Developing Your Intuition

"Nancy Marie has developed an effective series of exercises in which the resonance of the voice creates vibrational patterns that help to balance the human body and reduce stress. When this happens, the prefrontal cortex reactivates, our intuition increases and we function on a higher level."
Bruce Lipton, Ph.D. Cellular Biology
(excerpted from Foreword)

"I have worked with Nancy Marie for over six years and have been profoundly impacted by her guidance and teachings. Her new book sets forth her work in a more concrete form, complete with exercises, stories and wonderful illustrations. It has helped me in further developing my own intuition and reconnecting with my soul. I recommend it to everyone."
Michael Horst, Adjunct Professor
University of Southern California
Founder & CEO, InSpire
  (Integrated Strategic Planning in Real Estate)
Co-Founder, Shenoa Retreat and Learning Center

Andrew Weil, M.D. has placed a copy of *The Beckoning Song of Your Soul, A Guidebook for Developing Your Intuition* and its companion tape in his Fellowship Program at the University of Arizona Program of Integrative Medicine.

"*The Beckoning Song of Your Soul* is a must-read. Full of great stories and helpful exercises, Nancy Marie's excellent book will teach you to use your intuition in a practical, effective way. This book can change your life."

Erik Olesen
Psychotherapist, Speaker and
Author of *Mastering the Winds of Change*

"Nancy Marie has given us not just a book but an important stepping stone for inner growth. In accessible, unassuming language, using vivid examples and warmly calligraphed vignettes, she reveals and exemplifies to us the power of finely tuned, still observation towards the inner and outer worlds. From that firm point on, the tree of our knowledge can only grow.

Her voice is authentic, receptive, playful yet targeted. This book is inviting and freeing, like a garden walk."

Anca Hariton, Author/Illustrator
Butterfly Story and *Dandelion Adventures*

"Nancy Marie is a very gentle, knowing soul. I know because I have worked with her privately for many years. Her book is a reflection of her wisdom. What particularly impressed me was that unlike many forms of spiritualism she gives sensitivity to the body a primary place. It is not relegated to the back seat as something we reluctantly take along but do not respect. In this book she shows that the body tells us incredible things, besides telling us who we are. I was also impressed with the timing of the exercises. They passed so easily and gracefully that I hardly noticed the huge leap of faith that she was asking me to make. She is saying that intuition is more than just another way of gathering information but that it is what connects us to earth and Spirit. And that the way we receive their messages is through the subtle language of the body. Thank you, Nancy Marie, for putting what you know in book form so we can return to it whenever we need your soul's knowing."

Susan Sasso
Wildlife Rehabilitator

The Beckoning Song
of
Your Soul

A Guidebook for Developing Your Intuition

written & illustrated by

Nancy Marie

Published by Inner Eye Publishing
P.O. Box 559
Mt. Shasta, California 96067

Copyeditor: Karla Maree
Page layout and Design: Dana Conant, Quicksilver Productions
Cover and Design: Nancy Marie
Photo on back cover: Elizabeth Fenwick

Library of Congress Cataloging-in-Publication Data
Marie, Nancy, 1947-
    The beckoning song of your soul : a guidebook for developing
    your intuition / written & illustrated by Nancy Marie.
    p.   cm.
    ISBN 0-9660418-0-1

    1. Intuition (Psychology)—Problems, exercises, etc.   I. Title.
    BF315.5.M37   1998
    153.4'4—dc21   97-39687
                                                        CIP

Publisher will plant two
trees for every tree used
to produce this book.

Printed on acid-free recycled
paper with soy-based ink

Dedicated to my

Mother and Father,

for without them,

none of this would be possible.

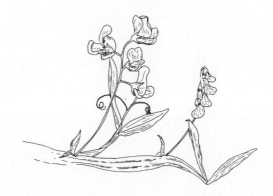

Acknowledgments

So many people have helped to make this book a reality, it would be difficult to mention them all, though I am deeply grateful for their encouragement and assistance. My heartfelt gratitude to both Karla Maree, my editor, and Dana Conant of Quicksilver Productions, my book designer, for their skill, knowledge, and wisdom. I would also like to express special thanks to Marion Weber for her ability to see and support the birthing of visions. Most of all I would like to thank my husband, Alan, and my children for their continuous belief in me.

Foreword

When I was seven years old, I experienced an event so dramatic that it set the course for the rest of my life. I was in second grade and our science teacher let us look into a microscope and observe a drop of pond water. At first I saw nothing but a blurred white field. Then a single-celled protozoan called a paramecium swam into the field. In the innocence of my child-mind, I saw this organism not as a cell but as a microscopic "person," a thinking, sentient being. While I was focusing on the paramecium, an alien-like amoeba began to ooze into the field. I was transfixed by these otherworldly creatures.

Twenty-eight years later I experienced the same thrill as I peered down the lens of an electron microscope, observing human muscle cells. As an Associate Professor of Anatomy at the University of Wisconsin's School of Medicine, my research was focused on understanding the mechanisms that control the growth and behavior of human cells.

Through my research, I realized a profoundly important fact: the structure and behavior of the human is very similar to that of the cell. In fact, although humans are comprised of from 50 to 100 trillion individual cells, we have no new "functions" that are not already present within the single cell. Because of this relationship, scientists are able to better understand human biology by studying cells.

Survival, in both humans and cells, is the result of two different types of behaviors: those that promote growth and reproduction, and those that protect the organism from threats on its life. Interestingly, a cell protecting itself cannot simultaneously engage in growth-promoting activities, and vice versa.

Thus a cell's physical structure and behaviors are responses to the environment. Its physiology, health, and behavior are primarily controlled by the "environment," or more specifically, its "perception" of its environment. The idea that organisms are shaped by their environment challenges the conventional beliefs of modern biology, which holds that organisms are controlled by their genes.

Later, while conducting research at Stanford University's School of Medicine, I published a study on the human immune system revealing that the environment did indeed control the expression of cells, even selecting the cell's gene programs. Eventually, I came to understand something that radically changed my life—the molecular pathways by which our "consciousness" controls the status of our cells, tissues, and organs. Our fears and stresses, whether they are valid or not, slow down our growth responses and can even alter our genetic programs. My research on cellular control mechanisms provided direct insight into the mind-body connection in humans.

I left academia in 1991 and since have been sharing this exciting new mind-body science with health practitioners and healers throughout the United States, Canada, and the Caribbean. The audiences especially appreciate gaining a scientific foundation to explain how our beliefs influence our biology. After every lecture, I am always asked if I have written a book. I usually say, "One is in progress."

The more pressure I put on myself to write the book, the more "writer's block" I experienced. My stress over this book finally impacted my own system. I woke up on a recent Saturday morning to find that half my face was immobile—paralyzed. I had contracted a condition known as Bell's Palsy. I went to my medical books and found that though there was no known cause or treatment, in most cases function is restored in eight weeks to six months. Unfortunately, I had a major presentation scheduled in less than four weeks and I could speak only with great difficulty.

The next day, Nancy Marie called to tell me about her new book. Seven years earlier, Nancy had been a participant in the first series of lay audience lectures that I prepared. Since that time, we have kept in touch. I knew Nancy to be an excellent psychic and asked if she might provide me with some insights that could help me come to grips with the palsy issue. This she did, and her explanation of my situation helped me to clarify my thinking and relax.

Several days later I received a copy of her book in the mail. It was beautifully written, simple to comprehend and a visual delight. The illustrations served as guided imagery that in themselves helped to reduce stress. Eagerly, I began to read the book. I realized that Nancy Marie had developed an effective system to help restore balance in the body. I used Nancy's exercises in conjunction with acupuncture and chiropractic adjustment and in two weeks my palsy was completely gone. I was also able to sit down at the computer and begin my writing in earnest.

Did Nancy's toning program contribute to my healing? On a scientific level the answer is clearly, yes! Research over the years has shown that chronic stress leads to heart disease, hypertension, depression, immune suppression, diabetes, neurodegeneration, and weight gain among others. Most recently, researchers have discovered that elevated stress hormones also affect the brain. When we're under significant stress, adrenal hormones trigger a part of the brain called the amygdala to recall habits used to cope with earlier (childhood) stress-related experiences.

At the same time, these adrenal hormones shut down the prefrontal cortex. This higher cognitive center of the brain normally allows memory to guide our behavior, inhibits inappropriate responses, and allows us to concentrate. (Both ADD and post-traumatic stress syndrome are associated with problems in the prefrontal cortex.) As famed stress researcher Hans Selye observed, stress prevents the nervous system from rising to a higher level of function.

And there's another way that stress impacts us. Itzak Bentov, author of *Stalking the Wild Pendulum: On the Mechanics of Consciousness*, says that "emotional" stresses are imprinted on the physical body just as music is imprinted on a phonograph record. According to Bentov, these stress vibrations can be enhanced, altered, or even eliminated by other vibrational patterns.

Nancy Marie has developed an effective series of exercises in which the resonance of the voice creates vibrational patterns that help to balance the human body and reduce stress. When this happens, the prefrontal cortex reactivates, our intuition increases and we function on a higher level.

That is why I practice some of the toning exercises from Nancy's book before I sit down at the computer to work on my own manuscript. The exercises help me to think better and feel more relaxed.

Thank you, Nancy. Your work has done wonders for my healing. And you've also given me a method to help my students bring their minds into harmony with their bodies.

Bruce Lipton, Ph.D., Cellular Biology

About the author

My name is Nancy Marie and, for lack of a better word, I am a psychic. Though I wasn't consciously aware of my abilities until I was in my late twenties, I've come to realize that I have always had heightened sensory abilities. It was in my late twenties when, one day, I had an experience that forced me to acknowledge that I perceived things differently from other people. Let me tell you what happened.

I was living and working in San Francisco at the time. On that particular day I was walking down the street to the restaurant where I worked. I was watching my feet as I walked and not paying attention to much of anything else, just deep in my own thoughts. For some reason I had an impulse to look up. What I saw nearly took my breath away. I was no longer seeing clothes or skin on the people I looked at; instead, I was looking directly into their bodies. Then—the most bizarre part—I saw "signs" in front of each person showing me what was ailing them. As I didn't know what was going on, I just kept looking down at my feet as I walked hoping that what was happening would stop. When I got to the restaurant, I focused on work because I couldn't talk to anyone about what was happening. As the evening progressed I became less frightened by what I was seeing and more fascinated by the phenomenon.

I began to experiment with what I was seeing, as if it were a game. For example, if I saw a sign that said "headache" on a co-worker, I would ask them how they were feeling to see if the sign was accurate. I still wasn't sure what was going on but was slightly less rattled by the end of the evening. When it was still happening several days later I decided I needed to break the silence and get some advice or help.

A friend suggested that I contact a very well-respected psychic in the area for advice. This felt strange for me because I had grown up in a conservative, middle-class, Catholic family. But, because I didn't have any other ideas of what I should do, I gave her a call. She became the first of many teachers who have helped me on my path.

In the first class I took I realized that my intuition had always been alive and functioning, I just hadn't been listening to it. It wasn't because I was stubborn or arrogant, only that no one had ever encouraged me to listen to my intuition or showed me how to recognize when I was getting a message from my soul.

You see, learning to understand your intuition is like learning a new language or learning to read music. It is quite easy once you learn to decode the system. But until that happens, it can sound or feel like a lot of jumble in your head. It can confuse you, and it can even make you feel as if you are going crazy.

About two decades ago the information for this book started showing up in my dreams and in my meditations. At first, I wasn't sure what I was supposed to do with the information, but as time passed, I found myself compelled to record every detail that I received. This was very unusual behavior for me, because I had never enjoyed writing before. Instead, I found myself obsessed with writing down every detail and doing the exercises in this book on a daily basis. Immediately, I noticed changes in myself. First, a deep inner calm and contentment seemed to wash over me as I connected more deeply with my soul. My intuitive perceptions became clearer and easier to express and I felt new joy and excitement for life. I was alive again! I couldn't remember the last time I had felt this revitalized. It was a wonderful feeling.

My friends and the people at the restaurant where I was working began asking what I was doing differently because they were also noticing the changes in me. "You look younger! You look happier! What are you doing differently?" they asked me. When I told my close friends about the exercises, they asked if I would teach them. I agreed. They, too, began to experience rapid changes in their lives.

This whole process of receiving information had been going on for a few years when I was approached by a woman I had never met before. "I heard about the exercises," she said. "Would you be willing to teach a class if I organized it?" That was the beginning.

That was twenty years ago. Since then, I have taught these same exercises to thousands of people, enabling them to reconnect more deeply with their own inner guidance. Six years ago I realized these teachings and exercises needed to be recorded in a book so they would be available to more people. You see, the stress and pressures of life create a need to be in touch with your intuition, if only as a way of maintaining sanity. For you who would like to embark on this journey, this book is my gift to you. My wish is that it will gently guide you to the place you seek.

At first glance, these exercises may seem simple; however, I have found them to be immensely transforming. They have had a profound effect on my own life. This approach to developing your intuition is different from other techniques because it is designed to help you shed those parts of yourself or your life that aren't harmonious with your spirit. When this happens, your natural intuition automatically blossoms.

In these last two decades, in addition to teaching, I have also done over 10,000 readings for people all over the world. I still use these exercises to strengthen my intuitive abilities, enabling me to access accurate information for people I have never even seen. I hope they can serve you as well.

How to use this book

I have pondered for quite some time as to when and how this book really became part of my life. After much deliberation I finally realized I've been writing it all my life. In my younger years, I experienced how difficult life can be if your intuition is not your constant companion. I would compare the experience to pushing your car up a steep, icy hill in the middle of a freezing blizzard—at night.

In my twenties, when I had the experience that sparked my transformation, I could no longer deny the existence of my intuition. Now after twenty years of walking with my intuition, I am aware of how magical life can be from this perspective.

Is there any practical reason to be in touch with your intuition, or is it just for spiritual development? Can having a good relationship with your intuition improve the quality of your daily life? Can it help you find a job or a partner that is really suited for you? Let me answer these questions this way.

When I was growing up I heard a lot about my mother's brother. He was a prominent efficiency expert. Companies would call him in to see where they were losing money and how to make their business more successful. To me, intuition is like an efficiency expert because it can show you where you are losing energy (or power) and how you can create a life that is more supportive of your spirit. You *can* get by without the assistance of your intuition, but I would compare the experience to walking down a dark tunnel, blindfolded with your hands tied behind your back and your ears plugged. In comparison, when you walk with the companionship of your intuition, it is similar to riding through the same tunnel in a comfortable car listening to some soothing music with your headlights on.

Life doesn't have to be as difficult as we sometimes make it. I grew up being told that life was tough and a struggle. So that is the imprint that my mind holds. On the other hand, when my intuition speaks to me I walk to another kind of music. It is like a floating, ethereal music that reminds me of the great pleasure and wonders I can experience just being alive. I have come to find that when I follow my inner voice, life takes on a more graceful quality.

This book was created for you. It was designed to help you reclaim more of your own sensory aliveness. This book is not for just reading. It works best with active participation. You will discover that the more you do these seemingly simple exercises, the deeper your understanding of your own intuition will grow. There is a great difference between just knowing something in your mind and knowing something with every cell of your being. This book is designed to help you develop the second kind of wisdom. For only with this second kind of knowing can real change take place in your life. So please, take the time to read the text, enjoy the illustrations, do the exercises slowly, and write the answers to the questions. This approach will help you to gain the fullest benefit of this book.

The Beckoning Song of Your Soul is really a collection of teachings, exercises, and stories woven together to create a path for you to follow. This is a path back to your soul and the voice of your soul, your intuition. The manner in which you each use this book might be slightly different. This is the way it is supposed to be. Follow the guidelines and make whatever personal adjustments you need to make—this your own personal journey.

Each section has information and exercises designed to help you open up in a certain way. Some sections you may find easier than others. This is because you have already developed some in that particular area of yourself. Other sections may be more difficult. Don't get discouraged, just give yourself extra time to get the most out of that section. Respect your own learning process. It is very important to start at the beginning of this book and progress systematically to the end, because each section is built upon the growth and understanding of the previous section. Sometimes you may feel like you are going down a blind tunnel. Just keep going and trust. You will see the light again. If, however, the confusion continues throughout the exercise, go back to the last place in the book where you felt surefooted and on track. Then proceed forward at a much slower pace. Most confusion is created by progressing through the material too fast.

Details and Suggestions

Blank Book

I recommend you either buy or make yourself a book with blank pages to use in conjunction with this guidebook. You will use it to record your answers, insights, and observations. Anytime you are asked to write in your workbook or 'Personal Journal,' do so in your blank book. I recommend blank pages because you will be using it for drawing lines and shapes in addition to writing.

Throughout this book there will be times where I suggest you write in your Personal Journal. The reason for this is to give you a chance to heighten your rapport and refine your communication with your inner voice. Repeated writing in your journal will also help you keep track of your insights, growths, and changes.

Toning

Early on in this book I use the word *toning*. I want you to know I am referring to the art of making sounds or tones with your voice for the purpose of creating a desired physical effect.

Grounding

Throughout the book I use the term "grounded" or "to ground." What I am wanting you to do is to stop and make sure you have solid footing or are solid within yourself. This is important because this work can open you up much faster than you might suspect. To maintain the full benefit of this work in every aspect of your life, each growth and realization must be fully integrated before you move on. This is also the reason I keep repeating, "take your time, slow down." This work can really fool you because it looks so simple, but the changes can be incredibly profound.

Interchangeable Terms

I use the words soul, spirit, authentic self, true self, and essence interchangeably throughout the book. If you have difficulty with any of these words or phrases, replace it with another word that is more acceptable. Sometimes it is hard to find words to express the intangible.

Questions

The questions asked in this book are designed to open up a conscious dialog between your body and your soul. So pay attention to the first answers that jump into your mind. Even if the response catches you off guard or seems out of character with the way you usually experience yourself, write that answer down. As time passes you will begin to gain a far more in-depth understanding of your soul and its inner wisdom.

Pace

If you allow yourself to follow the exercises at your own pace, repeating them as many times as you need and to reflect and answer the questions fully, you will find that subtle voice within you getting clearer and louder.

Intuition is a marvelous thing. It shows up in the most divine ways. It can give you suggestions or directions, though sometimes it might be difficult to understand the logic or purpose of an instruction. With practice you will become more accustomed to the manner in which your intuition speaks and will learn to follow and understand the purpose of its instructions.

What Can You Expect?

Healing can come in many forms. This material will penetrate and affect each and every one of you differently. Change will appear where there is imbalance in your life. The first impact of this book may hit your personal life or possibly your career. You will know it is working when you start becoming more aware of the things in your life that you need to change. Further use of this method will just spiral you deeper into a greater understanding of yourself and the meaning of your life. We as human beings have a great capacity to adapt for the purpose of survival. When we are ready to enter into our own healing, we must go through the process of removing behavior within ourselves that is not supportive of our soul. This can be painful and joyful at the same time. So be gentle with yourself.

Sometimes we are led to believe spiritual work is serious business, but I think the quickest path to your soul is the path of joy. (Have you ever seen a child do something they didn't enjoy for very long? Neither will your spirit, so make the process fun!) Laugh, dance, cry, and sing yourself back together.

Over the years, I've received many letters and phone calls from participants of my classes and workshops describing the changes in their lives. They have been my inspiration, propelling me further on my path. I welcome your stories also.

The Beckoning Song
of
Your Soul

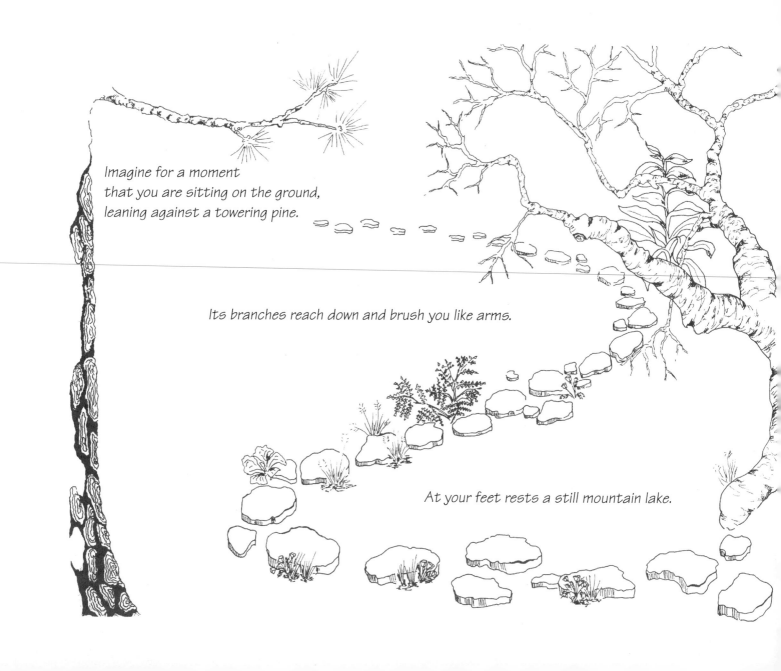

Imagine for a moment
that you are sitting on the ground,
leaning against a towering pine.

Its branches reach down and brush you like arms.

At your feet rests a still mountain lake.

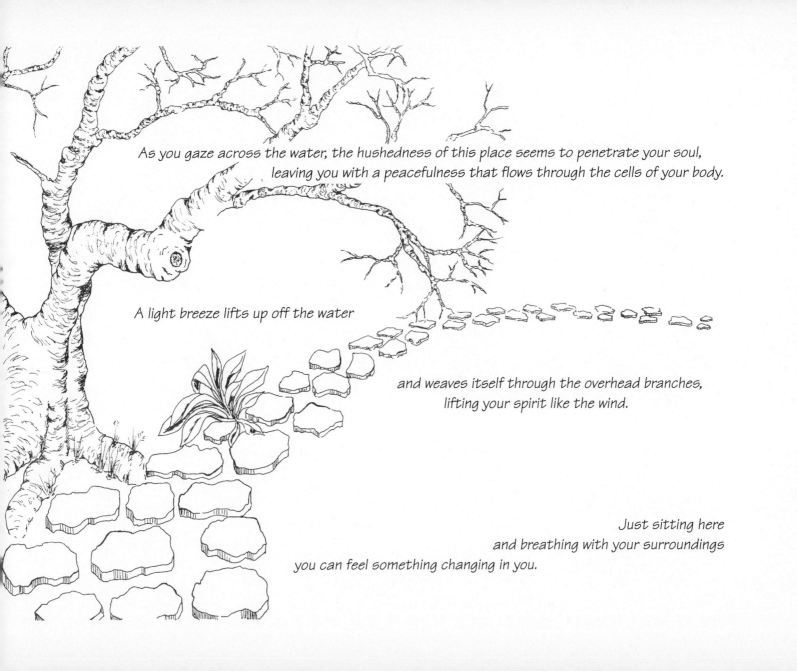

As you gaze across the water, the hushedness of this place seems to penetrate your soul,
leaving you with a peacefulness that flows through the cells of your body.

A light breeze lifts up off the water

and weaves itself through the overhead branches,
lifting your spirit like the wind.

Just sitting here
and breathing with your surroundings
you can feel something changing in you.

New energy and awareness
flows into your body.

Taking a deep breath,
you sink more deeply into the tree.

Your breath automatically slides into your lower belly,

while your vision seems to broaden with each inhalation.

You feel energized!

And at the same time
a sense of peace lingers inside your body.

You seem to be breathing with everything around you.

Time seems to stop.

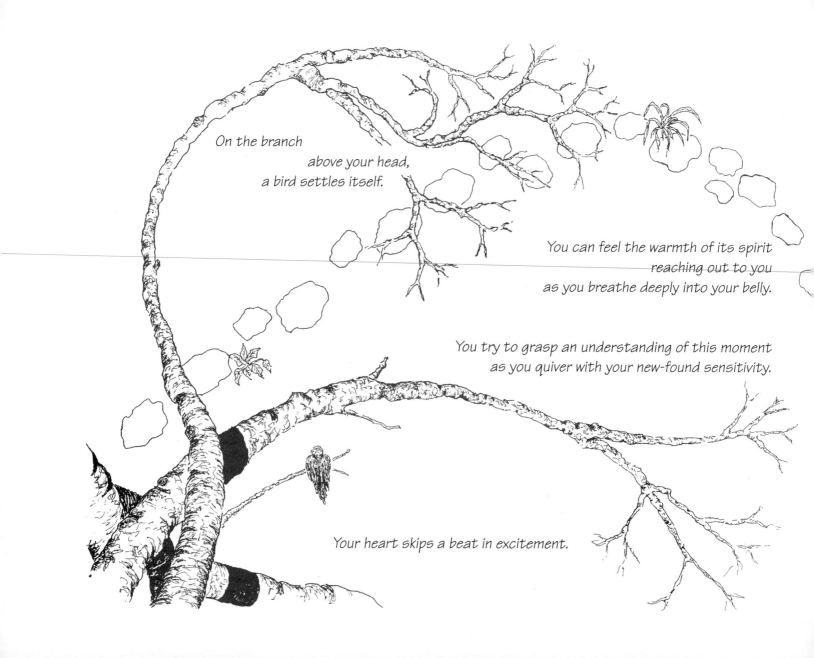

On the branch
above your head,
a bird settles itself.

You can feel the warmth of its spirit
reaching out to you
as you breathe deeply into your belly.

You try to grasp an understanding of this moment
as you quiver with your new-found sensitivity.

Your heart skips a beat in excitement.

You feel a sound wanting to float up from your heart
and out your mouth.

Will you allow this alignment with nature
to lift you out of your old self?

Or will you resist
and break the veil of this vibrational union?

The sound crosses your lips like a silent whisper.
But with your next breath
it sprouts wings and begins to glide on the breeze like a loose and wild leaf.

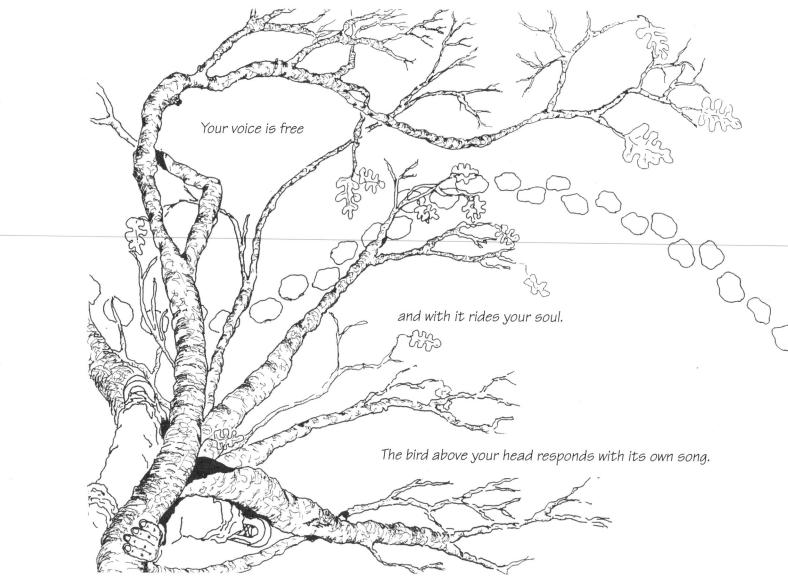

Your voice is free

and with it rides your soul.

The bird above your head responds with its own song.

Your soul soars as the juice of life pulses through your arteries and veins!

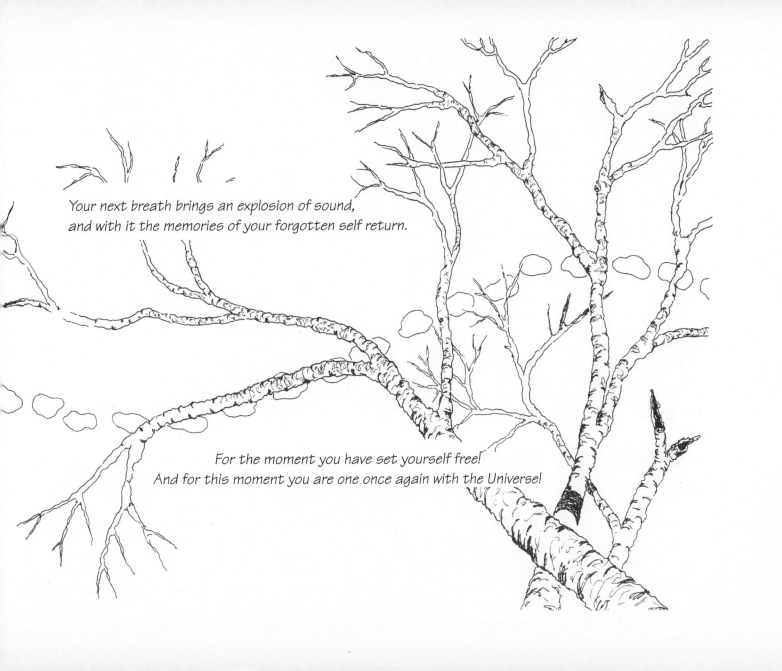

Your next breath brings an explosion of sound,
and with it the memories of your forgotten self return.

For the moment you have set yourself free!
And for this moment you are one once again with the Universe!

Connections

We weren't designed to be merely linear beings. We were born to be connected to all living things—a blend of body, mind, and spirit—though our lives today don't always support this union. Sometimes, though, you can have what I call a spontaneous realignment; when, for whatever reason, your body and spirit reconnect and you get to re-experience your wholeness. When this happens, you also get to experience yourself as an integral part of the Universe. These are sacred moments.

Unfortunately, many people spend much of their lives disconnected from their spirits and walk through life as distant and isolated observers. This is very sad, for when you disconnect in this manner you can lose touch with what is really important. Let me give you an example:

Lois lived down the street from me when I was a teenager. Whenever I walked by her house, I could see that she was always rushing around getting ready. Sometimes I would ask her what was she getting ready for. She would say, "Oh I don't know, but it's good to be ready." My mother said Lois spent all of her time cleaning and getting ready for visitors. I assumed that was so she could be with her guests when they came over for a visit. I found out that was not true, however, when my family was invited over to her house for dinner one evening. I figured that everything would be relaxed and organized because she had spent so much time getting ready. Was I surprised! She continued to bury herself with preparing the food and cleaning up afterward. The entire time we were there, she never once sat down and talked to us. It was like she wasn't there. It made me feel very strange.

When you fill your life with staying busy, as Lois did, it will be difficult to experience your wholeness and your purpose for being here. If you slow down, even a little, your spirit will reawaken. When that happens, then you are ready to work on developing a strong and vital relationship with your intuition, which can give you a richer sense of who you are and why you are here.

I have always found the voice to be a very powerful tool in the process of reclaiming your intuition. When you are using your voice properly, the mere utterance of any sound can center and ground you almost instantly. You will discover, from doing the exercises in this book, that when you make the sounds of your soul these tones will weave you back to remembering who you really are and your

place in the Universe. I know of no greater feeling than the bliss of knowing who you are and that you truly belong. A union and connection of this magnitude can give you the energy and confidence you need to pursue your dreams. But without this connection to your spirit, it is difficult to be fully alive and to make your dreams a reality.

Over the years I've been asked many times, "How can you know when you are disconnected from your spirit?" My answer is: If you have lost your hope or your direction, then your have lost your connection with your soul. If you have lost your ability to love or be loved, or are feeling overwhelmed and have lost your perspective on life, then you have lost touch with your spirit. If just being alive doesn't make you happy, or you are feeling hollow and empty, then you need to reconnect with your spirit.

If you feel you have lost touch with your spirit, do not despair. For I have found that through proper use of your voice, sound-generated movement, and imagery (which we focus on in this book), you can open yourself and reconnect with your soul quite easily. When this happens your intuition automatically blossoms like a flower. This experience can generate a deep sense of belonging within you because it puts you back in touch with life.

If you find yourself searching
for something to make you whole,
then I think you are indeed
in search of your soul.

4

Being Seen

First, we will focus on the development of the voice, because it is the sound reflection of the soul. Then we will add sound-generated movement, as this can unravel your chains of unresolved feelings. Finally, we will add imagery and art, for they can serve as a road map, leading you to the dreams of your spirit.

During the last eighteen years of teaching, I have heard thousands of people say "…they just don't see me…" when they are referring to a loved one or acquaintance. In most cases this is very true. What most people don't realize, however, is that they are part of the reason others can't see them. If you are generating your voice incorrectly, you create a false image or hologram of who you really are to the outside world. Then, when the outside world relates to that image, instead of seeing the real you, you feel unseen. The proper use of your voice can amplify or magnify your soul energy and secure it firmly in your physical body. When you use your voice in this way it is easier for others to see and experience your authentic self. Following is an example:

I met Linda, a twelve-year-old girl, through an art program I taught at her school. She was a very likeable child and many of the other children wanted to be friends with her, but she insisted on speaking only in baby-talk most of the time.

Since I worked with the children in small groups, I often overheard them talking about the situation. I was surprised by how openly they all discussed it. Some of the children said they thought it was weird, but most of them confessed that the baby-talk made them feel uncomfortable, because they didn't know how to respond to it. They wished she would stop it and just be herself, so they could connect with her.

It is impossible to connect deeply with someone if they are not connected to themselves.

Form

Physical form, as we know it today, is the result of vibrating sound. When the sound changes, the physical form also changes. When the sound generated by your body changes, the way you appear to the outside world also changes. This may not seem important, but if you are repeatedly having difficulty making your life work, you may want to look at what you are putting out to the world. The sound of your voice may be giving others mixed messages in the same way that Linda's baby-talk was confusing to the other children. Mixed messages are a kind of energy inconsistency. Inconsistency of this kind can create internal confusion in both you and those around you, thus making it difficult to make things happen easily in your life. It is confusing to know which part of you to relate to.

When people's bodies and spirits are connected, they are very comfortable to be around because the vibrations or sounds generated by the spirit and the body are harmonious—like listening to a beautiful symphony. There is no hidden agenda. In contrast, being around someone who is giving out vocal mixed messages is like listening to a radio that isn't quite tuned to one station. You keep getting bits and pieces of different conversations and songs. It is very difficult to follow and very exhausting to be around. Here's an example of what I mean:

About 22 years ago I attended a tai chi class given at a health club where I taught in San Francisco. I was very excited to finally be learning tai chi as it had fascinated me for some time.

At the beginning of the class, as Jeff talked about his teaching method, my body immediately began to tighten and my head to spin. I breathed deeply and told myself not to pass judgment and to give the class a chance. When we started to work on the movements, the sounds that were coming from his mouth were such a contradiction to the sounds that were coming from his body, I couldn't even follow him. I found myself tripping over my own feet and not even able to remember my left from my right. It really was like trying to follow a poorly tuned radio. All I could think about was how much I wanted out of that room.

Years later I was blessed by a wonderful tai chi teacher whose body and spirit pulsed to the same sound. Even in the first class my body seemed to move effortlessly. I was reminded once again that in the presence of inner harmony, learning and understanding are easy.

There are many ways a person can distort their voice, thus giving off mixed messages. These distortions usually stem from improper use of the mouth, throat, and diaphragm. One of the distinguishing factors is that the person's voice doesn't seem to fit them or it makes you uncomfortable and confused.

Following are three examples of voice distortion:

Marina was a performer, a beautiful woman who carried herself with great assuredness, and gave the external appearance of really knowing herself and where she was going. Everyone thought she would be very successful. I thought so too, until one day I got a chance to meet her personally. When I was introduced to her she extended her hand and opened her mouth to speak. Out came this little girl voice! It was very jarring. Her voice completely contradicted the image she was attempting to relate to the rest of the world. I remember standing there feeling speechless. I didn't know which part of her to relate to because I didn't know which part was pretend. It was very confusing. I also realized at that moment she wasn't going to be as successful as everyone thought.

She wouldn't be able to manage it with two contradictory realities going on at the same time.

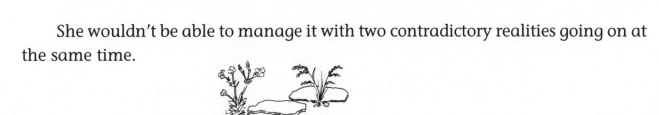

Early in her career as a therapist, Angela was so devoted to fixing others that she wasn't taking care of herself. She gave and she gave and she gave. You could hear the anger and resentment growing in her voice, but she continued to carry the image of the selfless nurturer. This situation began to cause chaos in both her practice and her private life. She was getting fewer and fewer referrals, and the clients she did have weren't improving.

A friend of hers finally pointed out that she was giving mixed messages. She was pretending to be a devoted caregiver, but the tone of her voice expressed her feelings of resentment and over-extension. She was presenting herself as someone who could help others put their lives together, yet she wasn't taking care of herself. Her voice had exposed the untruth. When she realized what she had been doing, she set out to make some changes in her life. Today, her practice and clients are thriving because she is taking care of herself. She says it was one of the best teachings she'd ever experienced.

It showed her how easy it was to give mixed messages.

Sister Mary Margaret was my eighth-grade teacher. I found her very confusing to be around. Her voice was sharp and her manner was incredibly short and intolerant. You couldn't get a word in edgewise because she was always right. When she talked it felt as if she were putting up a stone wall, holding us away with her facts and information. The impression we got from the sound of her voice made us feel that she didn't really want to connect with us, she just wanted us to obey. But the words she spoke said she wanted to get to know us, to be our friend.

At the time, it didn't make any sense, and, to this day, I can still feel the confusion of that situation.

These stories are just a few examples of distortion of the voice. What is important to remember is that any improper use of your voice can create a false image or hologram of you to the outside world, which makes accomplishing what you want more difficult.

Practice Time: Voice Distortion

This is your first opportunity to actively participate in this workbook. Before you start, close your eyes and take a few deep breaths to slow yourself down and to relax your body.

When you take the time to work with the questions and exercises in this book, changes in you will automatically be set in motion.

This is not a situation where fast is better. Take the time you need and allow yourself to receive the fullest benefit of this workbook.

When you feel you are relaxed and slowed down, turn to your workbook and answer these questions.

1. Can you remember talking to someone whose voice was distorted and they were giving you mixed messages? List up to three examples.

2. Write some words or phrases to describe how it feels in your body when you are talking to someone who is distorting their voice and giving mixed messages.

3. Can you remember a time when you distorted your voice and gave mixed messages? Describe the situation.

4. Can you remember how it felt in your body when your voice was distorted and you were giving mixed messages?

The purpose of these exercises is to increase your awareness of the wealth of information suspended in the sound of someone's voice. Learning to listen and pay attention to the way your body responds to someone's voice can give you a lot of insight about them and about yourself. This is also a great way to develop your intuition.

YOUR WORK FOR THE WEEK

- Listen to the voices around you during the day. Can you tell when someone is distorting their voice and giving mixed messages? What are your body clues?

- Can you tell when you distort your voice? What are your body clues?

13

Extra Insight: *Tape your voice when you are calm and relaxed and again when you are very stressed. Then replay it at another time and feel how your body responds to one sound versus the other. Write your observations.*

Theory

You may ask yourself why someone would not want to use their true voice? What would they gain from disconnecting from their soul or spirit in this way? Remembering the theory that form follows sound; let's take this theory a step further. I feel there is a moment in many children's lives when they realize that their parents are not able to see or embrace who they really are in spirit. This realization can cause great pain. In order to numb themselves to this pain they need to disconnect from their spirit. How do they manage to do this? By merely changing the sound of their voice. Remember, physical form follows sound. So by changing the sound generated by their voice, they force their body to vibrate at a frequency different from their soul's vibration and, consequently, their body and soul split and become separate. The form, or persona, of their physical body also changes because it is not in phase (or vibrating to the same rhythm) with their soul. When this happens they cannot move as one. Whenever you force your body or yourself to be someone you really aren't, your body and spirit automatically separate.

Up until that moment of the split, the child's body was patterned and directed by the internal sounds of their souls. This is known as rhythm entrainment. When the body and soul were still connected, this vibrational fascia also held them in alignment with the whole Universe. This is important to remember, because when you disconnect from your soul you are also disconnecting from the oneness of the entire Universe. This is why you experience such aloneness and isolation when you aren't connected to your soul. You haven't just lost yourself, you have also lost touch with the force of life.

Once someone has split from their spirit, he or she might struggle for years trying desperately to bring those lost parts back together again. Here's an example from my own life:

When I was growing up I spent many years trying to be someone that I wasn't. Every year, through junior high and high school, I created a new image and personality in hopes of finding myself. "This is the real me!" I would say to myself, but each 'image' would last only about a month before I would realize it wasn't really me. By the time I was in my early twenties, I realized that very little of what I thought I was, was me. Finally one day I set upon a crusade to find and reclaim that part of me I only had vague memories of. I tried many things over the years as I searched for myself. Then one day as I sat outside looking up at the trees, I felt a stillness breathe inside me. Within that stillness I could sense and feel a self I had forgotten. As I leaned back against my chair

I knew this was where I lived, within the stillness that breathed with the wind.

Your true voice is like home base; it feeds you and recharges your spirit. Suspended in its sound is the blueprint of your soul. When you disconnect from your true voice or soul sound, it's difficult to remember who you really are and why you are here. By teaching and training your body to vibrate, once again, to the sound and song of your soul, you can be one—not only with yourself, but with the whole Universe. This very small change can have a profound effect on all of your life. Once you start vibrating your body to the sounds of your soul, it will be almost impossible to live a life that is not supportive of your soul. Basically, it will be difficult to be in denial anymore. The story that follows reflects this awareness.

When I was in college I met an amazing man, Hal, who was also attending the same college. He was 82 years old, which was difficult to believe because I had never met anyone who was more alive than him. He was very active on campus. You would see him at almost any activity you went to. He was unbelievably vital. One day over tea I asked him what his secret to life was. He responded, with a twinkle in his eye, "I sing in the morning, and I dance at night. And I only do what I want to do. The other takes too much energy!"

Remember, it's like the flick of the magician's wand, the mere touch of the healer's hand. By changing your voice, you also change the image or persona of who you are. In the same way, a mere flick of your voice can change you back into who you really are. In doing so you reclaim your soul and your place in the river of life.

Can you remember feeling elated after jumping up and down and cheering for your team? Or maybe you've had the experience of going to a concert where the music took such a hold of you that you sang and danced long into the night? Perhaps you've had the experience of spending an evening with old friends where you laughed and spontaneously shared stories and memories with each other. In situations such as these we forget about who we think we are and let our energy and spirit fly. If you allowed yourself to get into the experience with gusto, you probably felt lighter and energized at the same time. The process of this book is designed to lift you out of your self-defined restraints and set your spirit free. So dive into this workbook with abandonment. For once your spirit is free, it is easy to gain balance in your life.

Toning is an Art

The first techniques you will use to reestablish your connection with your soul are sound or toning techniques. Toning, as mentioned before, is the art of using vocal sounds to expand and to reactivate your soul energy, thus increasing your life- force energy and your connection with the rest of life.

The fundamentals of toning are not something new, but are, rather, ancient healing tools. Their roots have been passed down through history and used by many cultures. The vocal techniques of toning are used specifically to open up and unblock the energy in your mouth, your throat, and your diaphragm, thus releasing a constant flow of energy throughout your body. In developing the intuition it is necessary for the body to be open and relaxed. Any constriction in the body can distort information you get intuitively. Tension in the body can also distort the sound of your voice, consequently giving others a false impression of who you are and what you're saying. While this might not seem especially important, it is this kind of vibrational distortion that can create chaos in your life. If you want to have harmony in your life, you can't be giving out mixed messages. You need your body to be open and fluid, without hiding or distorting who you are or what you feel. This kind of vibrational unity can give you internal harmony and a more joyful connection with life.

It's very easy to lose track of the life your spirit really needs. The woman in the following story got caught up in a web of life she thought she wanted. But when her real calling became evident, she was able to create what she had wanted all along but hadn't known how to find.

Many years ago I worked at a clinic owned by a woman named Alicia. She was there for everyone and had a heart of gold. For no visible reason, though, she was always in some kind of crisis. It was as if a cloud of chaos and confusion surrounded her at all times. If it wasn't money problems it was health problems. If is wasn't health problems it was relationship problems. As time passed it became more distressing and exhausting to be around her. Eventually her business failed even though she was good at what she did.

Several years later we bumped into to each other. I hardly recognized her, she was so different. She told me that after her business folded, she did some deep soul searching. She said she finally came to terms with the fact that she wasn't happy as a businesswoman and that her real loves were music and gardening. She decided to follow her heart. She was currently singing with a group of women and working at a nursery. "This is the life I was looking for," she

said, beaming. "I feel at peace and connected to life again."

"It's kind of funny," she continued. "I gave up what I really wanted to do because I felt I needed a stable life, and now that I'm connected to myself and doing what makes me happy, I feel far more stable than ever before."

Using the sound and breath techniques that follow can help you open up and regain your own inner stability.

Natural Breathing

As you lighten your load, your breath naturally drops into your lower belly. Breathing from this place automatically releases blocked energy. With this fresh movement of energy your inner sight will begin to open. Don't rush or try to push this vibrational shift. Let yourself breathe more deeply, for breathing from your lower belly is as natural as being intuitive. This is where peace and tranquillity live. This is where your primordial sense of knowing is birthed. This is where the deep kinesthetic sense of who you are lives like a sleeping dragon. This is where the fire of your force erupts. This is the place where you are one.

In order to bond once more with your intuition (the voice of your soul) and enter the web of your wholeness, you need to travel on the winding, spiraling, and breathing path that all of nature travels. You cannot return to your soul via the fast lane, and you can't get there by the analytical or linear ways of the world. Use your voice, your movement, and your imagery, for it is through these arts that you can find true passage to your soul. Remember, this is the journey to your Self—the journey of embracing who you are and taking your rightful place in the universe.

The story that follows is an example of the importance of proper breathing.

Back in the mid-seventies, I taught trapeze and acrobatics at a small studio in San Francisco. One day a 65-year-old man showed up at a class. Jonathan said he had always dreamed of being able to do acrobatics and to swing on a trapeze, but he had never been able to. He wondered if it was possible at his age. I told him I was willing to give it a try. We worked on his breath for a long time to get it fuller and more fluid. Once his breathing had dropped down into his lower belly, I was sure his body would be able to follow and learn the skills. We worked together for several months, making slow, gradual progress. When he finally did his first cartwheel, he turned to me and said, "I think I found the fountain of youth. It's in the breath! I feel like a kid again. It's a wonderful feeling."

When you find yourself breathing with a full belly breath, you will find that every inhalation and exhalation activates your intuition naturally. By nature, we were designed to be fully seeing, breathing and feeling beings. It is the stress, pressure and tension of our current society that actually perpetuates the disconnection from our intuitions and, consequently, from our spirits. And from that place of "spirit disconnection," it is difficult for us to stay in touch with what's really important. So slow yourself down and disconnect yourself, instead, from those things in your life that prevent you from being with you. Here's a story that illustrates how life's pressures can disconnect you from your Self.

About 15 years ago, Beverly, a very gifted graphic designer, attended one of my workshops. She told me she loved her work, but something was going on that she couldn't understand. She used to trust her intuition, but now for some reason she was doubting her every move. This indecisiveness was wreaking havoc on her at work.

When I looked deeper, I became aware that there had been some recent changes in her life. It seemed she had a new supervisor and was working in an environment she found very irritating. Beverly confirmed that this was true. She had been recently promoted and consequently had a different supervisor and a different office. "This is where your problem lies," I told her. She then divulged that her new supervisor yelled a lot and became negative when she was stressed. As for her new office, the walls were painted orange, which gave her

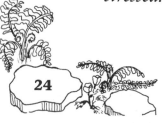

a headache whenever she looked at them. The more we talked, the more Beverly became aware of how the increase of stress and pressure at work was cutting her off from her intuition. The office was an easy change. She went in one weekend and painted the walls a soft eggshell blue. She also filled her office with lots of plants and a bubbling fountain so she would have a retreat. She discovered that once she identified the problem, she was able to disregard her supervisor's bad moods. Her only problem was that now everyone at the office wanted to hang out in her office because it was so soothing.

Exercise 1: The Breath

The purpose of this exercise is to expand and increase your awareness of your breathing. Full natural breathing is the foundation of toning. If your breathing is full, it will be easier to generate your soul sound.

Make yourself comfortable. It doesn't matter whether you're sitting or lying down, but your body needs to be relaxed. Close your eyes and place your hand on your lower belly. Inhale through your nose and exhale through your mouth.

Feel your breath fill your lower belly with each inhalation and leave your belly with each exhalation. If you have trouble getting the breath to be smooth, move your body into a more horizontal position. (It's easier for the body to return to its natural breathing patterns when it is lying down.) Continue for five to ten minutes. Do this exercise daily until your breath is smooth and relaxed.

When you have finished with this exercise, return to your workbook and answer the following questions.

(Remember there are no right or wrong answers—just the answers that pop out of you. Learn to trust your inner voice.)

1. Describe how your body feels after you do this exercise. Pay attention to subtle changes.

2. Can you tell when you are breathing fully?

3. What are some of the clues and sensations?

4. In what situations do you have more difficulty breathing fully?

5. In what situations do you find it easy to breath fully?

YOUR WORK FOR THE WEEK

- Do the breath exercise every day.

- Observe your breathing during the week, and record any observations in your Personal Journal.

- Spend additional time pondering the questions.

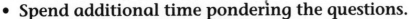

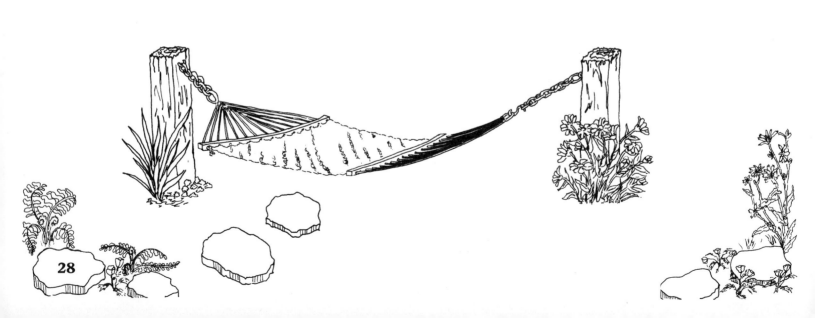

28

Toning

Toning is very different from singing. In singing you form and place your voice in front of your teeth for the purpose of creating a wonderful sound for the enjoyment and pleasure of the listener. Toning is for You. It is the art of using your voice to balance and harmonize your own energy. When you tone, you place your voice in the center of your mouth cavity. This placement of the voice stimulates your brain, allowing it to rebalance. From this realignment in the head, the rest of your body is encouraged and stimulated to rebalance. This kind of sound strengthens your awareness of your soul in your body. Here's a story of one person's experience.

From time to time I do evening presentations of my work. This particular evening I was giving a talk at a bookstore in California. I noticed the woman right off. She was sitting in the last row. Outwardly, she appeared to be a very bitter and rigid woman. But the energy of her aura told me a very different story. Throughout my presentation she never looked up; she focused only on taking notes, as if she was trying to avoid experiencing what was happening in the room.

After I had spoken for a while, I asked everyone to put down their pencils and pens so I could lead them through an exercise. The woman in the last row continued to take notes. I then explained, without directing attention toward her, that in order for everyone to benefit, everyone would have to stop taking notes for a while. The woman in the last row reluctantly put down her pencil. We then began the exercise. When we finished, I suggested that everyone keep their eyes closed for a few minutes so they could spend some quiet time savoring any new awareness they might have gained from the exercise. When the woman in the last row lifted her head, I saw tears pouring down her face. Then she spoke for the first time that evening. "I never felt my soul before," she said between sobs. "I never knew I was so beautiful on the inside," she continued. "I just never knew." Even though she was crying, her face now glowed from that inner radiance I had seen in her before. For the moment she had set herself free.

Technique

When you tone, open your mouth wide. The more you open your jaw, the larger the resonant cavity you make. The larger the cavity, the fuller and richer the sound and, consequently, the more powerful the effect it has on your body. Remember, the purpose of toning is to increase access to your intuition. The clearer the sounds generated by your voice, the more you amplify your soul. The more expanded your soul, the easier it is to hear it speak to you via your intuition.

When you start toning, sometimes your voice will sound tight, flat, and unpleasant. This is not your true voice but rather the sound of accumulated tension in your body. I call it the girdle of "should," because this tension comes from not being able to be yourself. If you do experience tension, continue with the exercises anyway. You will find that your voice—and you—will gradually open up.

Voice

Everyone has a beautiful voice because everyone has a beautiful soul. You don't want your voice to sound like anyone else's, because suspended in the unique sound and quality of your voice is all of your ancient knowledge and wisdom. When your voice is vibrating correctly for you, you naturally radiate this wisdom and the world gets to bathe in all of your wonder just by hearing the sound of your voice. Here's a story that illustrates this.

About 25 years ago, I attended a benefit concert at Kezar Stadium in San Francisco. It was an unusually hot summer afternoon and some of the crowd was drinking heavily. Halfway through the concert, fights began breaking out all over the stadium. Groups of people were running down the aisles beating up other people for no reason. One fight would ignite another as panic spread like a grass fire. It felt as if the whole stadium would erupt into a riot at any minute. Instead, a woman singer stepped out on stage and began singing a gospel song a capella to the 10,000 people. As the strength and clarity of her beautiful voice washed over the crowd, the fights literally dissolved. It was amazing to see the impact one voice could have.

Remember, everyone has a beautiful voice, because everyone has a beautiful soul.

Three Chambers

The main purpose of the next four exercises is to familiarize you with how your body is affected by and responds to sound. These exercises can also help you develop a deeper awareness of your subtle energy. The insights you gain in these exercises will serve as a foundation for the more advanced exercises. They are the roots from which your new awareness will grow. Take all the time you need with each exercise so you can gain a deep experiential sense of yourself.

The Body

The body is a three-chambered instrument. (In contrast, a guitar is a one-chambered instrument.) Each of these areas is stimulated or activated by different-pitched sounds. There is a head chamber, a chest chamber, and a pelvic chamber. Your head chamber extends from the cranial bone (top of head) to the palette (the roof of your mouth). Your chest chamber extends from your palette to your diaphragm. And finally, your pelvic chamber extends from your diaphragm to your tailbone. The size and shape of each chamber or area of your body affects the tone and resonant quality of the sound generated by that area of the body.

Head Chamber

When you send sound through the head chamber, you stimulate and evoke thoughts, ideas, images, and visions. The sounds that stimulate the head are the highest of the three chambers. If you have lost track of the dreams of your spirit, making sounds that vibrate this upper chamber can help you remember them once again.

Chest Chamber

When you send sound through your chest chamber, you stimulate your emotional or feeling body. The sound of your chest chamber is a mid-range sound, which serves as an emotional link between all living things. It is through this sound that you transmit your emotions and feelings to others. When you make the sound of your chest chamber you can also release suppressed emotions and heighten your emotional sensitivity. This healing enables you to connect and feel more deeply.

34

Pelvic Chamber

When you send sound through your pelvic chamber, you are vibrating your root sound and the source of all of your creation. This is the most powerful area in your body. You need to take care of its sacredness and be aware of its vulnerability. This is not something that our culture teaches us, so the use of toning, movement, and art to access this wisdom is very important. Within this area lies the seed and potential of all creation. This low sound has such a strong resonant quality that when it is vibrated fully it can stimulate and activate all three chambers of the body.

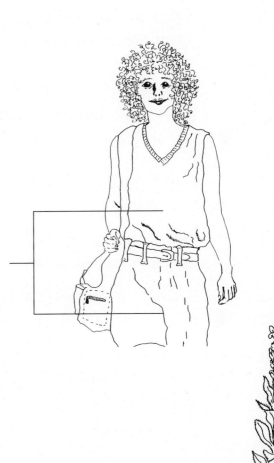

Practice Suggestions

Before we begin to practice making sounds, I want to give you some suggestions that can make these exercises easier.

- In toning there is no "right" note. Listen to your body and it will tell you what your head sound, chest sound, and pelvic sound are.

- Let the sound that rises out of you float out on top of your exhalation.

- Don't push your voice or it will constrict your throat and distort your sound.

- Remember: Deep within you, your soul sound is in its pure, original state. The real task is getting it out of your body without any distortion.

- If your throat tightens up, push your tongue in front of your lower lip as you would if you were making a "blah" sound. This will pull the tongue forward when you tone, releasing the throat or any tightness in your throat.

- Use vowels sounds only, because consonants interrupt the sound, depleting the vibrational effect on the body.

- In the vowel sound "ah," your mouth is the most open. It is for this reason

that I recommend you start toning first with an "ah." Then when you feel comfortable with toning, feel free to play with all the vowel sounds. They each have a different effect on your body. *Have fun with this exercise! Your intuition works better when you are happy.*

Exercise 2: Head Chamber

Just as in the previous exercise, make yourself comfortable. It doesn't matter if you are sitting or lying down, but your body needs to be relaxed. If you have a tendency to get chilled, cover yourself with a blanket. Place yourself in a room or outdoors, it doesn't matter. It does need to be somewhere that you won't be interrupted or inhibited, as you will need to have all of your attention focused inward.

Close your eyes and place your hand on your lower belly. Inhale through your nose and exhale through your mouth. Feel your breath fill your lower belly with each inhalation and leave your belly with each exhalation. If you have trouble getting the breath to be smooth, move your body into a more horizontal position, just as before. Your body can return to natural breathing with greater ease when you are lying down.

When you feel your breathing has taken on a full and relaxed pattern, it is time to proceed. Make sounds with each exhalation until you find one that will vibrate your forehead or the top of your head. This will be the highest of the three sounds. To keep from tightening up or changing your breathing pattern, imagine floating the sound on top of your exhalation.

Let the sound start out as almost a whisper. When you feel you have found one that vibrates or stimulates the center of your forehead or any part of your upper head you can slowly increase the volume.

Your mouth should be open. Lift you hand and see if your mouth is open. There should be enough space between your teeth for you to insert two fingers. If you can't get your fingers in, open your mouth wider. The more open your mouth is, the larger the cavity. The larger your mouth cavity is, the fuller the sound. The fuller the sound, the deeper and more profound the experience can be.

Keep making the same sound over and over again. With each breath, focus

on how your body responds to that sound. When you have made the sound enough that you have a clear sense of how it affects your body, you may move on to the chest sound. If you aren't sure if you have done enough or you have a tendency to rush things, make the same sound for at least five minutes.

When you have finished with this exercise, return to your workbook and answer the following questions.

1. Describe the sensations, reactions, or feelings you felt when you toned the sound of your head chamber.

2. Was it pleasurable or uncomfortable?

3. What insights about yourself did you gain by making this sound?

If you found vibrating the sounds of this chamber of the body pleasurable and easy to make, it indicates that this area of your body is already quite open. If you experienced difficulty or discomfort when you tried to make a head sound, it is probably due to tension or restriction in this part of your body. If that happens, just observe the tension or the restriction and don't judge yourself. Remember, just making an observation can set change in motion. Also, repeated practice of this exercise will lift tension out of your body, helping it open up once again. The purpose of this exercise is to open the body, enabling the intuition to flow naturally.

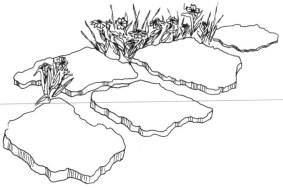

Exercise 3: Chest Chamber

Proceed with the chest sound in the same manner as Exercise 2. You will want to find a sound that vibrates your sternum (breast bone) or your rib cage. This will be a mid-range sound. Just as with Exercise 2, focus on keeping your body relaxed, your mouth open, and the sound floating on your exhalation. Never force or push because that will distort the sound. If you find emotions or tears rising while you are toning, don't stop the toning or the emotions; they can happen at the same time. Keep making your sound until you can feel its richness expand and fill your chest cavity. If you feel unsure of whether you've gone long enough use the five-minute guideline.

When you have finished with this exercise, return to your workbook and answer the following questions.

1. Describe the sensations, reactions, or feelings you felt when you toned the sound of the chest chamber.

2. Was it pleasurable or uncomfortable?

3. Did you gain any insight about yourself by making this sound?

If you find creating the sounds of this area of your body easy and pleasurable, it indicates that this part of your body is quite open. If you experience difficulty or discomfort making this sound or a lot of emotion arises, it is a sign of congestion or restriction. Once again, don't judge yourself, just observe. This alone will bring about change. You want to use this information to help you become more aware of

what's going on inside your body. (Don't ever use your observations to put yourself down. That will not be productive.) When you finish with the chest chamber, go to the pelvic sound.

Exercise 4: Pelvic Chamber

Some people are able to generate a pelvic sound with great ease, others have difficulty. If you have any trouble feeling or making the pelvic sound, repeat the head sound and the chest sound several times. The added vibration from these areas will help release some more body tension, making it easier to access the pelvic sound. Throughout the chamber exercises, remember that the goal is to become familiar with how your body responds to different sounds and to become comfortable with making a sound float on top of your exhalation.

When you make the pelvic sound, you are looking for a sound that stimulates your pelvic bone, genitals, or your lower abdomen. This will be the lowest of all three sounds. Just as in the two previous exercises, make sure your mouth is open and your body is relaxed. If at any time during this exercise you realize that you are uncomfortable, stop the exercise, resituate yourself and then continue. This is very important because if you are uncomfortable, your body will tense. If your body is tensing, it will be harder to get the lower sounds. Continue making the sounds of the pelvic chamber until you can feel some kind of change in that area. It could be a warmth or just a deep relaxing or opening up of the whole body. If you're unsure, you can use the five-minute guideline.

When you have finished with this exercise, return to your workbook and answer the following questions.

1. Describe the sensations, reactions, or feelings you felt when you toned the sounds of the pelvic chamber

2. Was it pleasurable or uncomfortable?

3. Did you gain any insights about yourself by making this sound?

Once again, if the sounds that vibrated this area of your body are enjoyable, it indicates that this part of your body is open. When you experience discomfort or it is difficult to create the sound of your pelvis, it indicates there is still too much tension in the body or restriction in the pelvic area. *Please be gentle with yourself.* For it is *only* through gentle nudging that your body will open. If you push or judge yourself, you will slow down your personal growth.

Personal Learning Journal

Take some time to reflect on and write about how your body responded to these last three exercises in your workbook before you proceed to the next exercise. Remember, writing about an experience can help you digest and integrate the new information.

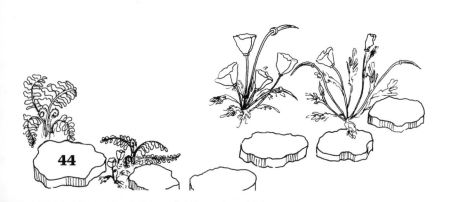

Exercise 5: Three Chambers

This exercise is really a composite of the three previous exercises. Before you begin, make sure you are physically comfortable. When you are ready to begin, start with the head sound. Make sure your mouth is open and with each exhalation let the sound of your head float out your mouth. Repeat that same sound over and over.

When you feel you would like to change sounds, drop down into your chest sound. Stay with this sound, allowing your voice to float out your mouth in its usual relaxed manner. After you have done the chest sound for awhile, you might feel like returning to the head sound. Once again, stay with that sound until you feel an impulse to go back to the chest sound or go on to the pelvic sound.

After you have done all three sounds you may stop or continue doing the head, chest, and pelvic sounds again until your body feels incredibly relaxed and satiated. This is a wonderful feeling, so I encourage you to continue until you have reached this point of pleasure.

One very important rule: **Always end with the pelvic sound. This will help ground and anchor you.**

When you have finished with this exercise, return to your workbook and answer the following questions.

1. How does your body feel after doing these sounds? Are you aware of any changes?

2. Which sound did you like the most? Why?

3. Which sound did you like the least? Why?

4. Which sound was the easiest to make?

5. Which was the hardest to make?

6. Which sound makes you the most peaceful?

7. Which sound lifts your spirits the most?

8. Which sound is the most energizing?

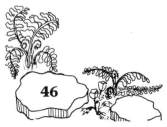

Many times, following the inner guidance of your intuition is like following the wind. You need to develop a rapport and sensitivity to subtleties. Learning to be aware of how your body responds to sound can help build that subtle sensitivity. These first five exercises were designed to help you become more aware of the subtleties of your own energy. Remember, they are the roots from which the other teaching will grow. They were created to turn the knob and begin to open the door to your greater awareness.

I recommend you take at least a week to focus on Exercises 2 through 5 (though you may take much more time if you want). When you're ready, continue on in the workbook.

YOUR WORK FOR THE WEEK

- **Do the chamber exercises every day.**

- **Observe the sound of your voice during the week in different situations.**

- **Spend time reflecting and responding to the questions.**

- **Write about any changes or reactions you observe in yourself in your Personal Journal.**

Bond

Since the onset of the Industrial Revolution, humans have been so focused on forging forward that they have lost touch with the concept of "oneness" with all living things. Without your connection with the pulse of life, you lose your connection to your intuition, your spirit, and the real meaning of life. Our society, with all of its pressure and striving to dominate, does not value this bond. As a result of this devaluing and ignoring our basic human need for connection with life, we continue to grow further and further away from our intuitions and our souls. These connections are crucial because without them (intuition or soul), life becomes a dry, meaningless experience. However, with a renewed connection to your intuition and your spirit, you breathe once again with the earth and the pulse of life. This bond will reawaken the powers and wisdom that lie dormant within you.

This bond can be reawakened in many ways. The story that follows is about a woman who played a major role in keeping that aliveness within me.

When I was very young we lived in an apartment house. The lady who lived upstairs from us was a wonderful spirit who filled her apartment with plants and great smells. We called her "Grandma Upstairs." Almost every day my sister and I would climb the stairs to her apartment to pay her a visit. We enjoyed her company because she was so much fun to be around. She would always tell us stories and let us mix up all kinds of ingredients to make a cake. Then, before we left she would promise to bake it for us. (I can't imagine what those things really tasted like, but she always apologized when we returned the next day because she had eaten the whole thing.) "It was so-o-o good," she would say with a smile. Grandma Upstairs always told us, "Life is like making a cake. You add a little of this and some of that and, presto, you have something very good. Always add lots of sugar if you want to make it sweet," she would tell us, pointing her finger at the bowl. To this day I can still remember how good it felt at her apartment. I rarely wanted to go home, but when I did I was always overflowing with joy. I realize now, when I look back at this memory, that what I was attracted to was her aliveness. It was so sweet to be around.

We all need sweet aliveness in our lives, because we were not designed to move through life alone or to handle our daily trials and challenges without any vibrational support. When we breathe as an integral part of the whole Universe, we don't experience isolation but rather can glide through life with a greater ease.

This alignment or partnership with life can give you the strength to understand and reclaim the lost fibers of your soul. All of life is much easier to delve into and deal with when you aren't overwhelmed with a debilitating sense of isolation. Note the following story:

Several years ago I had lunch with my friend Susan in San Francisco. From the outside, Susan's life with her husband and three children appeared almost perfect. That day over lunch Susan confessed that she felt hollow and empty. She said she was happy with everything in her life, it was just that something was missing. She was getting worried because some days she didn't want to get out of bed. The more we talked, the more it became clear that her whole life was about following things external to her. And that she didn't really know how to connect with herself. That conversation took place in the spring. Somewhere late in the summer she called again. The first thing I noticed was the spark in her voice. Life seemed to bubble out of her mouth. When we met for lunch later that day, I wasn't ready for what I saw. She looked about ten years younger and the cloud of depression had lifted. Energy radiated off her body as she moved with a new fluidity. It seems that after our conversation she had spent some *time trying to remember things that made her happy. She remembered the magic she had experienced in dancing and singing when she was a child. So she decided to study dance and to sing more at home just for herself. As a result, many new doors were opening for her. She told me she hadn't realized how isolated she had become until she starting doing something that made her so happy.*

It is easy to get so caught up in our external responsibilities that we lose touch with what makes our spirit sing.

Roots

The songs, chants, dances, rituals, and stories of our ancestors are the things that have always carried our cultural heritage to us, reminding us of our genetic roots and connections. But few of us have much in our personal lives that performs the same sacred function for our spirits. Our spirits need their own songs, dances, and images to remind us of who we are and why we are here. We need simple techniques that we can use in the mainstream of our daily lives to keep us bonded continuously to our spirits and to the breath of life.

Children naturally sing the song of their souls and use their bodies and minds to maintain that connection throughout their daily life. Through the interactivities of this workbook, you have the opportunity to reconnect with the forgotten songs, dances, and images of your spirit, and to weave them into your daily life once again. Here is a story about my father's way of staying connected to his soul.

Throughout my whole childhood I watched my father get up two hours early almost every day to spend time in his garden before heading off to work. You could see him puttering around in the yard in those early morning hours talking to his trees and singing to himself. These morning hours were filled with his rituals. Nature was his sanctuary, his retreat, and his healer. It was through his connection to his trees and plants that he was able to maintain his equilibrium and find his inner peace.

What do you have in your life that reminds you of your vibrational roots? Remember, this is the point of this work. You are in the process of learning simple techniques that can help you return to yourself even during times of stress, pressure, and confusion.

Practice Time: Review

This exercise will help you remember the song of your soul. Many ancient cultures believed that you did not know yourself until you could sing your own song. When you sing your melody, you are suspended in a state of knowing. It is in this place you can remember with great ease who you are and what is important to you.

Before we go any further please flip back and review the list of suggestions on page 36.

Exercise 6: Progressive Toning

As in the previous exercises, make yourself comfortable before you start. It doesn't matter if you are sitting or lying down, but your body needs to be supported and relaxed. If you have a tendency to get chilled, get yourself a blanket. Place yourself in a room or outdoors where you won't be interrupted or inhibited. It's important to take care of the body in this way so all of your focus and attention can go inward.

In the previous exercises you were limited to three sounds, the head, the chest, and the pelvic. Starting with this exercise you will find yourself wanting to use a larger range of notes. Trust that impulse and your song will begin to unfold.

Close your eyes and place your hand on your lower belly. Inhale through your nose and exhale through your mouth several times to help bring your attention even more inward. When you feel you have slowed yourself down and settled into yourself, you may continue.

To begin, open your mouth in the proper way and make the highest note that is comfortable for you. Now, repeat that note over and over until you can feel your body wanting to make a note that is either higher or lower. (You will literally feel a physical sensation in your body, indicating the need for a change and guiding you to make the next higher or lower note.) But what do you do if you don't get that

guiding sensation? Stay with the same note. At some point your body will want you to make a different note. Stay relaxed and watch for internal clues. When you get a clue, make that note over and over until you can feel your body wanting to make a different note that is either higher or lower.

If you had a piece of sheet music in your head, you would be able to see the beginnings of your soul melody emerging. Relax and enjoy the process. Each time you do this exercise you will be able to pick up more of the subtleties and nuances of your song and in the process gain a greater understanding of yourself. Remember, we are sound before matter. When we allow the fullness of our sound to be expressed, then our form can reflect that growth.

How will you know when you are done? The same way you know you are full when you eat. When you are satiated. When you don't want to make any more sound, then you are done. Follow this exercise one note at a time until you feel yourself filled with an inner stillness or fullness.

Sometimes when people first start toning, they find that tears start to roll when they tone. Allow this to happen. Don't stop toning and don't stop the tears. Your body is just releasing. When those old tears have drained out you will feel a lot lighter. This exercise usually takes between five to fifteen minutes. If it takes longer, don't fret, just sit back and enjoy the journey. This is *not* something you can—or should—rush. This is not a situation where faster is better. Remember, no one else in the whole world will have the same melody as you because no one else in the world carries the wisdom that you do. When you learn to play your song, the whole world will benefit because we will be able to hear and experience more of you and the wisdom you carry.

When you are done you will have the feeling of internal satiation. But say you have done some head notes, some chest notes, and some pelvic notes and then you have returned to chest notes—and at that point you feel a sense of completion. ***Before you finish, you need to make sure that you finish with at least one low note, the lowest note you can make.*** This is the grounding note, the note that says "the end" or Amen.

After you finish this exercise, keep your eyes closed for at least a minute and reflect on any changes that have transpired.

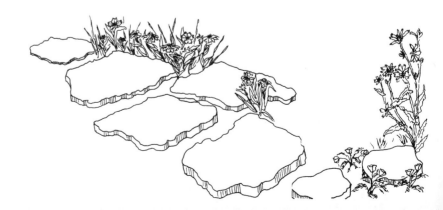

When you have finished with this exercise, return to your workbook and answer the following questions.

1. What did your melody sound like? How did singing it make you feel?

2. What sensations or images arose while you sang the beginnings of your song?

3. How do you feel about your song?

4. How did your body feel when you finished your song?

5. Was it difficult or easy to follow your internal clues?

6. How could you tell when to go up or down?

7. Do you remember your body feeling this way before? What was the situation?

8. While toning your song did you experience any insights or realizations of

YOUR WORK FOR THE WEEK

- Do the exercise daily.

- Spend some time responding to the previous questions.

- Discover at least five different places you feel comfortable toning because it is important to integrate this work into your daily life.

- Record changes that you notice in yourself in your Personal Journal.

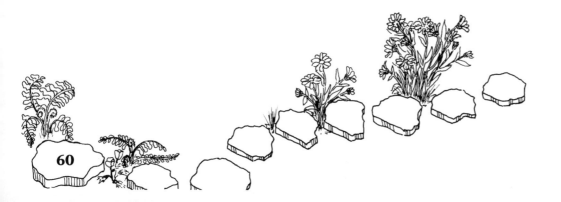

How well you are able to follow your internal clues in this exercise is a good gauge of how developed your intuition or subtle awareness is. If you had any difficulty doing this exercise, repeat it at a slower pace. Slowing it down will give you more time to look for clues. Remember, your intuition can talk to you in many ways. That is why it is important for you to come to understand the ways of your own intuition. Repeating this exercise daily will quickly heighten this awareness. In addition, each time you repeat this exercise, the nuances of your melody will arise and expand.

When you feel you can do this exercise with agility and your melody has developed a full-body richness, you may proceed to the next exercise. There is no need to rush. Take all the time you need with each exercise, repeating it as many times as you need to have a firm grasp of its teachings before you move on.

Society

If you had grown up in a society or community where everyone was encouraged to freely express themselves, either verbally, vocally, or creatively, you would grow up with a deeper sense of who you are and why you are here. You would also be innately more comfortable with who you are and, in turn, would extend the hand of acceptance to others. But this is not the world where most of us grew up. Many of us were not seen, valued, or appreciated. For us, this was not a world of safety or acceptance. In order to fit in, many of us had to hide who we were, the truth of what we saw, or how we were being treated. The mere hiding of your truth can distort the sound of your voice, giving mixed messages to those around you. Yes, the mere act of holding back the truth can change the sound of your voice, creating a "pretend you" for the world to see, and hiding your real self from the world. The main problem with this is that it makes your truth inaccessible to you as well. The larger the secret a child has to hold inside, the more inaccessible their true self becomes. This is because the tension created in the body to hide something from those outside constricts the breathing and speaking apparatus. This constriction distorts the sound of the voice, which in turn distorts or give a false image of who we really are. See the story that follows.

When I was growing up, my mother constantly told me how great our family was. She continuously painted a picture of our life, trying to make us believe it was perfect. The only problem was that our family life wasn't anything like the picture she painted. Not only that, I constantly felt pressure to maintain that false image to the outside world. As the years passed I became so absorbed in maintaining that false image I began to believe it to be true. In the process of living the lie, I lost the final crumbs of myself. By the time I was nineteen, I was so confused inside I felt crazy. I couldn't remember who I was or what was important to me. I was so crippled by the lie I was unable to create a healthy life for myself. This whole situation left me feeling trapped and alone.

When the teachings in this book began to enter my life, they were truly the answer to a prayer. They helped me reclaim my true self and understand why living a lie made me feel so crazy.

Practice Time: More Toning

Repeat the progressive toning exercise, then answer the following questions.

1. Can you remember being able to speak your truth when you were a child? Describe the situation.

2. When you were growing up, were you heard by anyone? Who? How did you know they heard you? What was their response?

3. If you think back to that moment, can you remember how it felt in your body?

4. Do you have any memories of wishing you could disappear? How did it feel in your body?

This process is not about making anyone wrong. It is about learning to vibrationally release old patterns and ways of being that are not in harmony with your spirit. When you are able to do this it is easier to embrace your future with open arms.

Now let's look at your answers for a moment. If you remember having some difficulty speaking your truth as a child, observe your voice carefully. You may be creating some voice distortion in your current daily life, which might not seem important, but it does make it more difficult to get what you want. To double-check this possibility, go back and review your answer to how your body felt when you couldn't speak the truth. Then fast-forward into your current life and ask yourself if you experience some of the same sensations in your body. If the answer is yes, remember that repeated practice of these exercises can change your vocal distortion patterns and, consequently, change your life.

YOUR WORK FOR THE WEEK

- Continue practicing the progressive toning.

- Take the time to note in your Personal Journal how being able to or not being able to speak your truth affects your daily life. (Remember, just becoming aware of something can set change in motion.)

- Did you learn anything new about yourself by answering these questions? Write your response in your Personal Journal.

Your Voice

As previously stated, toning can help you reopen your throat and mouth cavity and relax your tongue and diaphragm so that the sound generated by your speaking voice is the true sound and vibration of your soul. When this happens, you are bathed in the memory and the knowing of who you are every time you open your mouth to speak, sing, or utter sound. The smallest utterance of your voice can be a healing antidote to previous painful situations. This can be extremely useful in times of stress, since you always have your voice with you to help you reconnect with you.

As you breathe, you sound.
As you sound, you move.
As you move, you see.
And as you see,
you are.

The form, shape, and size of your whole being is the outgrowth of your original harmonic or soul sound. Your unique soul sound vibrationally carries all of your wisdom into your daily life. That is why when you sing your song you can have a profound understanding of your Self. This way of reconnecting with your intuition, through your wholeness, is very gentle and natural. Your song can create a place of great peace for you. In that space you stop struggling with your Self, and simply enjoy being alive.

Here's a story about a wonderful couple who lived this wisdom.

When I was in college my neighbors were an elderly couple who had lived their entire life in that small town. They had both worked at a small factory in town most of their lives. If they hadn't lived next door, I might have never had the opportunity to know them. I used to sit on my back porch after classes and watch them. There was such a gracefulness about the way they moved as they worked in their yard. It was almost as if they were propelled by their laughter. In the evening, as I did my homework, I could always hear their voices drifting across the lawn as they sang together. I can remember being mesmerized by them at times. How could they be so full of life? They possessed few

of the things I was raised to believe were valuable. One day I got up the courage to ask Fay. She laughed and said, "Didn't your mother ever teach you to sing, child? Don't you know singing makes your pain go away." I didn't know what she meant then, but I do know now.

When we sing our soul songs, we join the choir of life. From this place of tonal alignment we are able to see, feel, and access knowledge and wisdom beyond our usual senses. This heightened sense of aliveness is how our bodies are supposed to work all the time. It is our human heritage to be awake and integrated. The story that follows shows how simple vocalizing can soothe the soul (yours and others').

When I was young——back in the days before seat belts——I loved to stand behind my father when he drove the car. It was my favorite place in the car, because whenever my father would drive, he would sing. He had a deep voice and I found it very soothing. I would stand there, with my head and hands resting on the back of his seat, gazing out the side window. To this day, if I close my eyes, I can still feel his voice transport me to what I used to call my "wonderful dreaming place." It was like floating on a fluffy cloud or gliding on the

wind. When I was there, I would see and know things. They would just pop into my head. It was a wonderful experience. We can all take ourselves there now with our own voices.

Practice Time: Remembering Support

Take some time to answer the following questions.

1. What are your memories of vibrational support for your spirit? (Regardless of how large or small, if you are still here, they had to exist.)

2. Do you remember how it felt in your body when you did get support? (Use these memories to strengthen yourself.)

3. Do you remember how it felt in your body when you didn't get support? (This is a good thing to remember, because if you get that same feeling in your daily life you now know where the feeling comes from. It will be telling you that you currently aren't being supported.)

72

Movement

Learning to follow and understand the way your body moves in response to your sound can accelerate the communication between your body and spirit. Every organ of your body has a sound or voice and is able to speak to you. When your understanding of the language of your body becomes more sophisticated, you can translate what it's trying to tell you into a linear manner. This is a way to consciously stay in touch with your soul and address the needs of your physical body.

Every movement is a sound at its origin. We move unknowingly throughout our lives to the external sounds around us. But when we are strongly connected to our souls, we are guided and anchored by the rhythmic pulsation of our original sound more than by external sound.

In the following exercises focus on feeling, hearing, or sensing the sound that is the impulse for your movement. You want your own sound to create your movement. That is the way you were designed to move most effectively. This will prevent you from moving or being controlled by external stimulation. Moving to external sound does not nourish your soul in the same way as moving to your own sound. It can also take life feeding energy from the body and leave you depleted instead of revitalizing you. When your body moves from your soul sound, it also ignites your intuitive awareness. From this place of aliveness, your body becomes a fluid paintbrush. Each movement shows you another aspect of yourself.

Learn to follow your every move! By watching and sensing in this manner, you can learn to understand what your body is trying to tell you. We aren't talking about huge, grandiose movements, but rather small, subtle movements that originate from either your breath or sound. Pay close attention so that your movement really does originate from either your breath or your sound.

The story that follows is about a teacher who introduced me to the art of breathing.

I was in my late twenties when I took my first tap dancing class. The teacher, Mr. Wong, was a small, extremely fluid Oriental man. I had never seen anyone move the way he did. It was as if he was made only of liquid. At

the time it boggled my mind. As I continued to study with him I began to feel the same fluidity also move into my body. I didn't know how he was accomplishing this magical transformation in me, because everything seemed so calm and natural. One day I stayed late to ask him his secret. He just smiled and said, "You're breathing right for a change. That's the difference."

In order for the body to be open and fluid like a paintbrush, we need to be breathing in a full and relaxed manner.

Practice Time: Adding Movement

The purpose of this exercise is to help you see and experience how your body organically responds to the sounds that you create. Pay close attention to the level of grace and fluidity present when you move from your soul sounds versus external sounds. This level of awareness will help you detect whether you are moving from your soul sound or external sounds in your daily life.

Begin by linking your sounds together in a progressive toning, just as you have done in the previous exercise. As your sounds begin to fill your body, like air filling a balloon, let yourself experience the energy of those sounds flowing through your torso and limbs, creating subtle movement. Keep your focus inward and your eyes closed. It will help you really follow your sound and the movement that it's creating. Remember, we are looking *only for movement that is birthed by your sound.*

If possible, stand up for this exercise. However, if you have any difficulty standing up, you may do this exercise sitting or lying down. It will not detract from your experience.

Since you have done Exercise 6 (progressive toning) several times, you should be relatively comfortable with making the sounds of your melody. You don't need to be an expert to proceed, but being comfortable with making your sounds will help you focus primarily on the movement. This will give you a greater sense of

freedom, and make this exercise more fun. Trying to focus on both creating your sounds and following the movement will be too stressful, so if you're not comfortable with making the sounds of your melody, please wait to do this exercise until you are. You will then be able to focus all your attention on the subtle movements of your body, thus creating a far more powerful experience.

Exercise 7: Adding Movement

Close your eyes and place your hand on your lower belly. Inhale through your nose and exhale through your mouth several times to settle yourself into your body.

When you're ready, start with the highest comfortable note as you did in the previous exercise. Your destination is the lowest note possible (just as in Exercise 6). Allow the sound to build inside you. Then there will be far more force for your body to follow.

With each exhalation or sound, try to feel and sense how your body wants to respond. Imagine that your body is a balloon. With each exhalation let your body dance and bounce on your wind.

Keep everything small, slow, and subtle so that your attention is pulled inward. This will help you respond to your internal sound or breath.

Proceed with the toning in the same manner that you did in Exercise 6, paying attention to *all* the moves your body makes, no matter how small.

When you feel finished and satiated, remember to end with at least one low note. This will help ground the experience. Keep your eyes closed for a moment so you can absorb what has transpired.

When you have finished with this exercise, return to your workbook and answer the following questions.

1. Describe how your body felt when it began to move to the sounds of your soul. Is that different from the way you normally move? Explain.

2. What part of your body moved with the most fluidity? Which part was least fluid?

3. How do you know when you are following the internal direction of your own sound? What are your clues?

4. In what situations is it easier for you to follow the internal direction of your own sound?

5. Did you learn anything new about yourself as a result of this exercise?

6. What are some of the ways you can apply this information to your daily life?

Remember, there are no right or wrong answers. The reason for these questions is to help you focus on what is happening inside your body. Obligations and responsibilities can burden you to the point that you lose touch with yourself. Hopefully, some of these questions will help you reconnect the threads that hold your soul and body together.

YOUR WORK FOR THE WEEK

- Do Exercise 7 every day.

- Spend time answering the questions.

- Observe how your body responds to the sounds you create and those created by others in your daily life. Record observations in your Personal Journal.

- Observe whether your body responds more to the sounds you create or those created by others. Record observations in your Personal Journal.

- Once you have become comfortable with doing this exercise, begin using it as a tool to reconnect with yourself at times of stress.

When you are ready, proceed to the next exercise. Remember, there is no rush.

82

Imagery

In addition to sound and movement, you're also going to use imagery and art to help you reclaim the voice of your soul. Art and imagery can create a road map for your mind. When your mind gets a clear picture of where you want to go or changes you want to make, you can move far more efficiently. This translates into less stress and less frustration in your life. It also means that change can come more quickly.

In rendering the image of your soul, you will use the form of the circle, because a circle has no beginning and no end just like your soul. The image of your soul is birthed from watching the lines and shapes your body draws when propelled by the sounds of your soul.

Think back to the last exercise. Can you remember a way your hand or even your fingers moved in response to your sound? If you can imagine that your limbs are pencils, it might be easier to see the lines and shapes they make as you sing your song. Once you're able to see these lines you can then take up your pencil and draw them on paper.

Since you are going to see these lines in your mind when you do the exercise, you don't need to open your eyes to draw their simple pattern on your paper. In fact it may be preferable to keep your eyes closed, because it will intensify your

focus and bypass any performance anxiety you may have about drawing. Remember, there is no right or wrong here. This is merely a process by which you can pull the threads of your soul together once again. The key is just to focus on the movement and the lines drawn by your movement.

You don't need to be a great artist to draw the image of your soul. You just need to watch and see yourself.

Practice Time: Reflecting Your Soul

The purpose of this exercise is to learn to take the lines drawn by your body when it is moved by the sounds of your soul and convert those lines into an image that holds at least a part of the vibrational reflection of your soul. The more you allow yourself to play with this exercise, the easier it will be to truly grasp the fibers of your being on paper. When this happens it is truly an amazing experience. *Remember, you do not need to have any previous drawing skills.* You just need to focus your attention enough to see behind your veils. When you do, you will be able to create a design that holds and reflects back a part of you.

The drawing of your soul image is a process. It is not something that can be forced or rushed. You need to let it unfold. It may come quickly or it may come slowly. Think of it as a flower blooming. Allow the images to draw themselves.

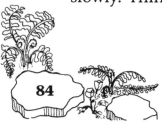

Then their meaning will also naturally unfold to you. When you have captured your soul image on paper, just viewing it will realign you and transport you back to the time when you were one with your spirit and the Universe.

In the process of drawing your soul image, you'll find that pieces of you will begin to slide together. You may experience this as "flashes," pictures, and/or sensations in your body. No matter which way these pieces return, record them as best you can. Make a habit of recording these puzzle pieces of yourself immediately, even if it is only a line or a shape with no words. As you record these images you're bringing parts of your whole being back together again.

Preparation

If you are able to stand, do so in this exercise also. Leave your workbook open to a blank page so you can easily transcribe the information that arises from this exercise. When you are finished with this exercise, stay deep within yourself, so you can walk back through the experience and collect any lines, patterns, or shapes that you feel are important. Open your eyes only slightly, still holding onto the experience. Then try to draw those lines in the way you saw them in your mind. Ask yourself, what is important? Is it the color, the shape, or the line? It may take you several times doing this exercise before you can grasp the filaments of your soul. But finding even a crumb can be exciting.

Exercise 8: The Reflection of Your Soul

Now close your eyes and get comfortable in the same manner you did in the previous exercises. Then imagine that your limbs are pencils or paint brushes. As you move, envision the strokes or lines that are created by your body.

Place your hand on your lower belly and inhale through your nose and exhale through your mouth several times to settle yourself into your body. When you are ready, start with the highest note you can comfortably make, just as you did in the previous exercise. As the sound begins to build inside of you, watch your body respond with subtle stretches and moves. Continue to allow the fluidity and rhythm of your sound to propel your body.

When you feel finished and satiated, remember to end with at least one low note. This will help ground the experience. Keep your eyes closed for a moment so you can absorb what has transpired.

When you are ready, please turn to a blank page in your workbook and record any lines, shapes, or images that you saw or felt during this exercise (examples follow).

Example I

Imagine your arm wanted to move in a circular motion. You might end up with a line that looks like this.

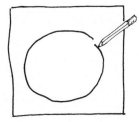

Example II

Perhaps your fingers kept wanting to move in a rotating manner. Your lines may end up looking like this.

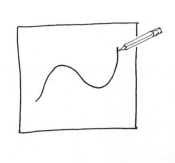

Taking an experience and trying to record it on paper can take practice. But every time you repeat this exercise, you are developing your sensing and focusing abilities, which are pertinent to the blossoming of your intuition.

YOUR WORK FOR THE WEEK

- Repeat these exercises daily.

- Observe the lines and shapes your body creates in your daily life.

- Write your observations in your Personal Journal.

Exercise 9: Rendering Your Soul Image

Now it is time to take these seemingly simple lines that you have been drawing and begin weaving them together. For this process you will need some supplies:

- a pencil and an eraser

- tracing paper

- a ruler or straight-edge

- a compass or something that will make a circle (a plate or bowl)

- coloring materials (felt pens, color pencils, water colors, pastels or anything you like)

Being able to add color to your image is important. The more you do this exercise, the more aware you will become of the kind of color you are looking for. Some people need the bright, strong colors from felt-tip pens, while others respond to the subtleties of colored pencils and watercolors. There is no right or wrong, just what feels right for you.

Remember, this is a process. Merely by doing the exercises, you can bring yourself more in touch with your inner voice.

Now turn to where you have recorded the lines and shapes drawn by your body in Exercise 8. Take a piece of tracing paper and place it over the lines and shapes and trace them with a pencil.

Example I

From page 87, the lines created
by arm movements:

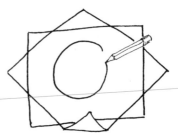

Example II

From page 87, the lines created
by hand movements:

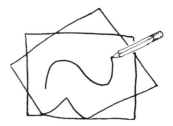

Now, draw a large circle on a piece of blank paper like the one below. You will need to put a black dot in the center of the circle to use as a guide.

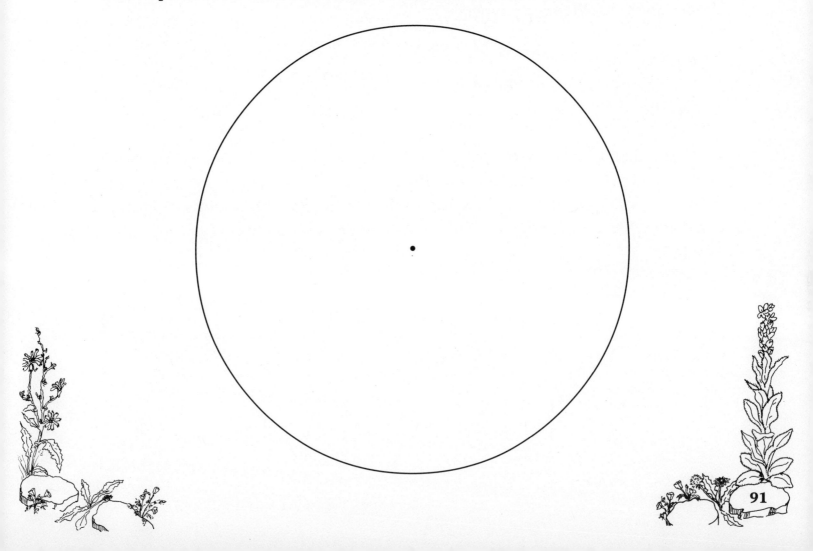

Turn the tracing paper over and rub the lead of your pencil over the back of your drawing creating a carbon paper.

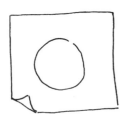 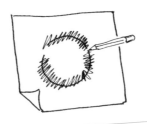 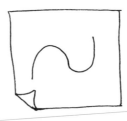 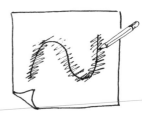

Turn the paper rightside up again. Position one of the lines you want to work with in the circle and retrace the line. The pressure of your pencil will get the line onto your paper (see circle 1). Now lift off the tracing paper and place it down in another position (see circle 2). Continue with your experimenting (see circle 3).

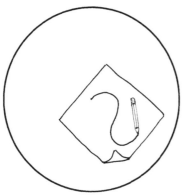 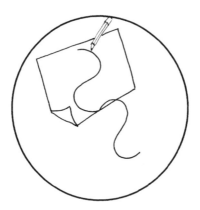 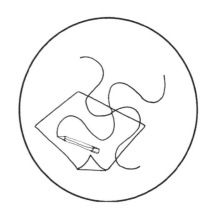

Repeat the line as many times as you want and in any pattern that feels right. Because you are using pencil, if you put down a line you don't like, just erase it. Play with and experiment with other shapes and lines if you want to. *Remember, trust how you feel and how you respond to this image.* No one else can tell you if it is right, only you. Don't lock yourself in by trying to do it right. Instead play with any ideas as they pop into your head.

Some people will have an immediate sense of how to link these lines together and other people will have to experiment. You might play with this exercise for days or even weeks before something really gels. **Remember, all the time you put into the process is a way of bringing those forgotten parts of yourself together.** So do not rush.

Here's an example of an image that was created using only one shape line (⌒). See how the drawing progressed from four lines to eight lines and finally to a very intricate drawing, all from one shaped line.

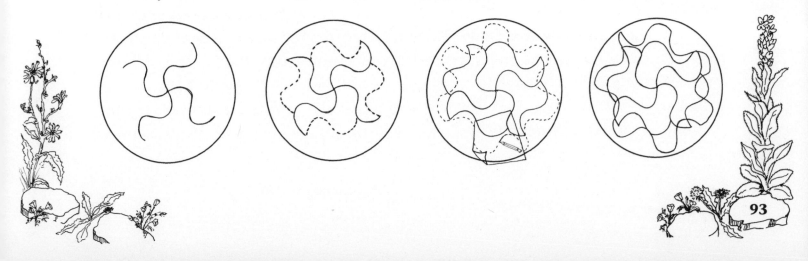

Below is an example of another image that was created by the same shaped line (∩∪). Notice how different they are, even though they were created from the same shaped line. This is why experimentation and sensing what feels right is important. Only you will know if the image feels right.

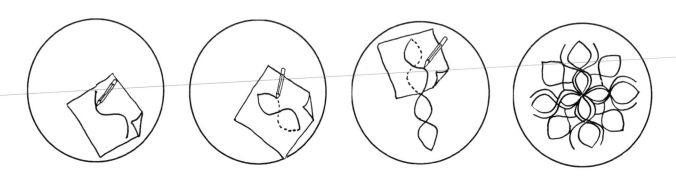

At some point a design will emerge. How will you know if you got it right? By the way you body responds to it. If, when you look at the design that has emerged from the lines drawn by your body and you feel inspired, you have definitely captured some of your essence on paper. Even if the response isn't that strong, still ask yourself how you feel. Gauge it on a scale of one to ten. Ten being best and no response would be a zero. If you rate yours a zero just repeat the exercise again. Remember, **this is a process**. If you have given yourself even a two or a three, it is a definite indicator that you are connecting with some of your vital energy. Good work!

When you hit that stage of development (a two or a three) use your image to teach you. This is how to proceed. Redo Exercise 8 paying very close attention to the lines and shapes your body draws. Then sit with your previously drawn image and observe where you have captured your essence and where you have not.

It might be in something as subtle as the thickness of your line. I reworked one of my designs for a long time before I discovered that the lines I was seeing were really like ribbons. The minute I realized that, the drawing took on a whole new dimension.

Remember, it is in the process of repeating the exercise and then reviewing what has emerged that we birth ourselves—not just on paper also in our daily lives.

If viewing your image creates warmth or pleasure inside of you, it is right. If the viewing of this image calms you or leaves you with a peaceful feeling, then it is right. This process is about reclaiming you, so trust your physical responses. If you feel it isn't right, do the exercise over. Work and play with the lines until they fall into place. Don't make yourself wrong! It will happen! Sometimes it just takes more time. *It is the repeated inward focusing and watching your physical clues that rebuilds the communication line to your soul.* That line of communication is your intuition. So it doesn't matter if it takes you three times or thirty times to find your soul image. It is the doing of the process that will rebuild those communication lines. Also, remember to have fun! Intuition works much better when you are light and happy.

Color

Some people take to color like fish take to water. Others feel apprehensive or are downright timid when it comes to adding color. Do not panic! There is always a safety net.

After you have worked on your design and you feel really good about it, but you are unsure what kind of color to use, go back and look at your notes. Did you ever see any color when you were doing the exercises? If so, that is a good place to start. But maybe you don't know where to put the color or what shade to use. This is what you do. You can photocopy your drawing many times and then experiment only on the photocopies, which eliminates the fear of ruining your original. Or you can just place tracing paper over your drawing and color only the tracing paper—you don't even have to redraw your lines. If you don't like how it turns out, just throw away the tracing paper and start again. Also repeating the toning with movement (Exercise 8) and focusing on color is also helpful. Just remember, it is easier to access your intuition if you are in a playful mood. At some point the waters will part as they did for every other stage. Just give yourself time and have fun.

98

Insights

Over the last 20 years of teaching, many of my students have written me and shared the changes that have transpired in their lives as a result of this work. These stories have always served as an inspiration for me. I'd like to share several with you, as they illustrate some of the main ingredients necessary to maintain a rich awareness your soul. The first is a copy of a letter I received several years ago.

Dear Nancy Marie,

"I grew up in a very abusive, alcoholic home. When I was little, I remember seeing my older brother and sister get beat up quite regularly by our father. It didn't take much to make him angry—drunk or sober. The mere act of voicing a different opinion was enough to start the yelling and beating. I can still remember the day that I decided to become invisible. I was five years old at the time. I was sitting under the dining-room table watching my father go after both my sister and brother. There was so much screaming and yelling, it made my body feel sick. Something inside me snapped that day. I can remember making a promise to myself. I didn't care what it took, I was never again going to be my father's beating post. So I became invisible. I never asked for

anything. I never voiced an opinion. And I never challenged anything that was said. Becoming invisible became my survival ticket. The only problem was that eventually I forgot who I was. I had been so focused on avoiding the brutality at home that I really lost touch with my own feelings, opinions, and ideas. As soon as I was old enough to leave, I moved out and married a man who was just like my father. But I didn't see it then because I had forgotten to think for myself and to voice my own opinions. My life just seemed to continue, and I survived once again. For years I never complained, and never asked for anything. Then one day my husband just up and left me for another woman. At first I was stunned and felt nothing, and then I found myself upset over little things he took with him without ever talking to me. It was about then that a friend talked me into attending your intuition workshop. I wasn't thrilled about attending, but once again I didn't know how to say "no."

Somehow a cloud seemed to be lifted out of me that day. It was a good feeling, so I continued doing the exercises daily. Gradually small changes became visible to me. Then, about three weeks later, I realized I wasn't the least bit distraught over the fact that my husband had left. In fact, I was quite overjoyed. You see, I suddenly realized that this was the first time in my life that I

was free to do things my way. I was free to be me! Well, I took on the challenge at a fevered pace. I got rid of anything I didn't like or that no longer had any meaning to me. I proceeded to fill my life with classes and adventures that really excited me. One day I was walking down the street and I bumped into an old friend. We talked for a while about this and that. And then she asked me if I missed my husband. I laughed and said "No, I have myself! And that is much better!" Thanks for helping me find myself.

With a smile on my face and a song in my heart,

Leslie

Leslie discovered the first important ingredient, the importance of having your Self. Life is always much better when you have your Self. Please remember this truth, it will greatly enrich your life.

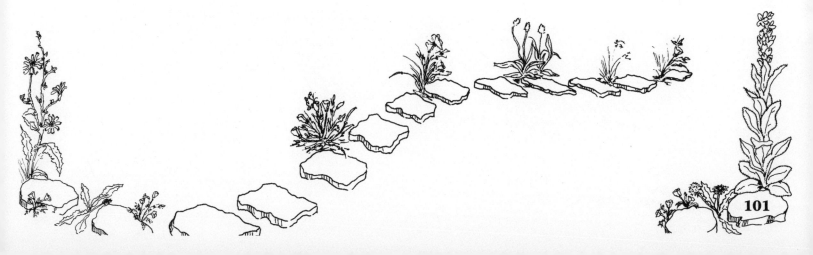

The second story I want to share with you is about a woman named Rose. Her story is a constant reminder to me that any growth or change you make, no matter how small, can have a profound effect on others:

Rose was a single mother who attended a weekend intuition development workshop about fifteen years ago. She was devoted to her two small children. She had attended the workshop because she felt she needed some new skills or techniques to help her be more sensitive and in touch with her children. During the whole weekend Rose was very focused and worked very intently on all the exercises. By the end of the first day I could see the stress and strain of her life melting away. Her skin was softer and her laughter became lighter and more spontaneous. Even her body appeared lighter and more carefree. It was great to see the metamorphosis.

On the second day of the workshop we usually talked about practical applications of the exercises. It was then that Rose divulged that she was very worried about her son, Kenneth. He was going to be kicked out of kindergarten if he didn't learn to manage his temper. She didn't know what to do. It seemed that his anger was ignited with very little provocation. She personally had experienced so much release and joy from the exercises the previous day she hoped that the changes in her might help him. I suggested that she teach him how to make the sounds and explain to him that it would take off the pressure when he was feeling upset or frustrated.

Six months later I received a phone call from Rose. After the workshop, she went home and used the techniques for a couple of weeks without saying anything to Kenneth. One day after school he asked her how she could be so happy. That was the opening she had been waiting for. She sat down and told him about the workshop and how she had learned to do sounds with her mouth that made her frustration and unhappiness go away. "Can you teach me?" he asked. Rose related that she was so happy at that moment she could barely keep back the tears of joy. That afternoon she taught Kenneth how to make the sounds. She wasn't ready for him to grasp it so quickly, but that evening a fight started at the dinner table between Kenneth and his younger brother. (It was their worst time of day because everyone was tired.) Suddenly, Kenneth asked to be excused. "I'll be back in a minute, mom," he said, and ran to his room. From behind the closed door she could hear him making sounds. The emotion that swelled up inside her was almost more than her chest could hold. Ten minutes later he saunters out with a smile in his eyes and grinning from ear to ear. "It works!" he proclaimed. And with that, he sat down and finished his dinner.

Kenneth is doing much better in school, Rose said. He told her that whenever he feels the explosion building, he finds a quite spot and make his sounds until he is able to remember what is making him so mad.

As an after-note, Kenneth has also taught his younger brother, who is four, how to make the sounds, as well as several of his friends.

Focus on developing your Self, as Rose did. Over time, the changes in you will become apparent to others just as the changes in her became apparent to her son. When the time is right, share your new-found growth and insights with your friends and loved ones, so they can also benefit from your blossoming.

This story illustrates how important it is to follow your heart:

Dick attended an eight-week intuition development program I taught about ten years ago. At the first meeting he was very quiet and withdrawn. The eight-week program worked in a manner similar to the workbook. I would teach an exercise at our weekly class time and then participants were required to practice all week and to keep track of their progress. It was about the third week that I noticed some changes in Dick. I had given an assignment to apply a technique to their personal life.

As background, Dick was the co-owner of a small software company. He and his brother had started the business about eight years before and it had mushroomed overnight. He really hadn't anticipated it growing as large as it had. In fact, part of him wished it hadn't gotten as large as it was. He loved the work, but he was overwhelmed with managing six employees.

When it was Dick's turn to talk about what had been happening with him during the past week, he exploded like an overripe fruit. The words were coming out of his mouth so fast he could hardly keep up with himself. It was amazing to watch. Here was this quiet and very inward man exploding with passion about how he loved designing software. How, when he was in that place, time just seemed to stop for him. He was sucked into a void where he was floating, with this energy just flowing through him. He could stay in that place for hours, for days, maybe even weeks. He didn't need to eat or sleep. It was the greatest high he had ever known, and he just loved it. He then talked about how doing the sounds had taken him back to that place that he so dearly loved. And not only that, when he was there, the sounds had somehow showed him what needed to change in his life. "I hate managing my company! And I am horrible at it, because I don't want to be doing it. I don't know how I'm going to do it, but come next week I plan to be a full-time designer," he enthused.

That was only week three. By the eighth week, Dick and his brother had hired a manager who would oversee the flow of the business, so both Dick and

his brother could both return to full-time designing. They also made many aesthetic changes in the office surroundings to enhance the relaxation and creativity of all the workers. The biggest change, however, was in Dick himself. He now knew that in order to be truly happy he needed to do things that made him happy. When we last spoke he said he still does his toning daily, to make sure that nothing slips through the cracks.

Let these stories remind you to follow your heart; to share what you have learned with others; and, finally, to remember that life is always better when you have your Self.

108

Where Do You Go from Here?

The exercises in this workbook may be done many, many times. In fact, the more often you do these exercises, the deeper your awareness of your spirit will grow. I recommend that you do the progressive toning with movement every day and work on drawing your image at least once a week. As you grow and open up from the progressive toning you will be able to see, feel, and experience far more of your soul image. With those changes, your image and sense of yourself will gain more depth and richness, sometimes on a daily basis. With each new awareness that you gain, changes (small or large) will happen in your life. Sometimes they will happen almost like magic. Other times, you will see something that needs to change, but also needs a little nudge from you. Nudge it! Remember, this process is not just about reconnecting with your spirit but also about creating a life that supports your soul and its path.

In closing I'd like to tell you a wonderful story I heard years ago:

It's about a woman who wanted to lose some extra weight she was carrying because it was preventing her from having the kind of life she really wanted. Even though she wanted to lose the weight, she wasn't able to stop eating the things she knew she shouldn't eat. So she went to the doctor to see if he could help her. He had her fill out a record of everything she had eaten in the last week. When he saw the record he said, "Here's your problem. You can't possibly lose any weight eating french fries, milkshakes, and cheeseburgers everyday. It just isn't possible." "Well, I know that's the problem," said the woman. "But try as I may, I haven't been able to give them up."

So the doctor said, "How about giving up only part of it?" "I think I can do that," said the woman.

The first week she gave up french fries. The second week she gave up milkshakes. The third week she gave up cheese on the burger. Now, the fourth week there was a problem, because the doctor wanted her to give up the bun and she said she couldn't, but she could give up the burger. What she discovered in this whole process was that she really only had a craving for the hamburger bun. She was eating all the other stuff with her hamburger bun only because that's what she'd been raised to do. You didn't just order a hamburger bun. That was strange! That was different! So instead, she let external voices dictate her choices and in the process she was unable to have the life she wanted.

After having done the exercises in this book you might also discover some french fries and milkshakes in your life that you need to shed. Let go of them with abandonment! Let go of those things that you no longer need. Hang on tight to what is really important.

As the story continues, the woman let go of the french fries, the milkshakes, the cheese, the lettuce, the tomato, and the mayo and lived happily ever after with the one thing that gave her warmth, nourishment, and a deep sense of her Self.

Ordering Information

For additional copies of *The Beckoning Song of Your Soul*, you may contact your local bookstore or order directly. A companion tape to be used in conjunction with the book is also available.

Order Form

Name _____ Phone (____) _____

Address _____

QTY.	ITEM	PRICE	TOTAL
	The Beckoning Song of Your Soul	$18.00	
	Companion Tape	10.00	
	Shipping & Handling ($3.00 for 1st book; add $1.25 for each additional item)		
	Sales Tax (orders shipped in California, add 7.25%)		
	TOTAL		

Make checks payable to Nancy Marie. Mail orders to:
P.O. Box 559, Mt. Shasta, CA 96067